"This is a most enjoyable and informative boating guide. We are relatively new boaters; just purchased our boat this past summer, and we live fifteen minutes from the Rideau. Next summer we plan to travel by boat from Manotick to Seeley's Bay with our two teenagers. This book will lead to improved preparation for our trip, clearly understood responsibilities for those aboard, and it will be less likely that we will need Family Counselling at the end of the voyage.

In spite of all the details to consider...Ya, we still wanna go!"

—Doreen and Ray Garrett
New Boaters

"An interesting and informative 'Bible' for all 'Rideauphiles'. It exudes useful information and most of all, a loving enjoyment of Colonel John By's 'Ditch'."

—P.A. Noel,
High School Instructor

"A wise and witty companion for the novice Rideau navigator. I'd rather by up the creek without a paddle than without Gray's instructive book."

—J.T. Boehm,
Diplomat

"Although written about the Rideau, its lessons apply equally to other Waterways, such as my cruising ground, the Trent-Severn, and the Erie Canal. Very informative in a light-hearted way."

—R.S. Coryell
Yachtsman

"I enjoyed your manuscript very much. Your sense of humour, coupled with the accurate, pertinent information and advice are an excellent vehicle for the message, 'Safe Courteous Boating Can Be Fun'. Budding boaters will find Rideau Navigator an informative introduction to the pleasures and the responsibilities of cruising on our waterway, without being bogged down by cold documentary language. If every navigator had a similar attitude and respect for the Rideau, its enjoyment by future generations would be ensured."

—D. Horsfall,
Len's Cove Marina

"There is nothing, absolutely nothing, half so much fun as simply messing about in boats—simply messing", explained rat to mole in <u>Wind in the Willows</u>. How true that is! So the cruising man's senses stir whenever he picks up a book which seeks to tell him of new adventures to undertake, around the world or in one's own backyard. I began my own cruising career 40 years ago with a voyage from Toronto to Parry Sound via the Severn River System. How I could have used this informative volume. Like a marriage, a voyage should not be undertaken "lightly" and this volume will help the expert as well as the novice be sure of eventualities.

As befits a man with 24 years in the Canadian Coast Guard, Doug Gray wants to be sure we have got it right before we begin, and what better advice can you get? Well you can get it with a touch of humour, a quality much needed when everything seems to go wrong. So use this excellent guide to be prepared and enjoy all the fun that boating in all its guises can offer.

—Fredrik S. Eaton

The
Rideau
Navigator

Going Down the River, Not Up the Creek

Doug Gray

Published by

GSPH GENERAL STORE
PUBLISHING HOUSE INC.

1 Main Street Burnstown, Ontario, Canada K0J 1G0
Telephone (613) 432-7697 Fax (613) 432-7184

ISBN 0-919431-65-8
Printed and bound in Canada

Cover Design and Layout by Leanne Enright

General Store Publishing House gratefully acknowledges the assistance of
the Ontario Arts Council.

Canadian Cataloguing in Publication Data
Gray, Doug (Robert Douglas), 1940-
    The Rideau navigator: going down the river, not up the creek

ISBN 0-919431-65-8

1. Rideau Canal (Ont.)--Navigation. I. Title
GV776.15.05G73 1993 623.89'2297137 C93-090045-6

Photo Credits:
1. Canadian Parks Service
    Rideau Canal Collection S. Lunn
    Cover Photo: David Flatman
2. D. Gray

First Printing March 1993

CONTENTS

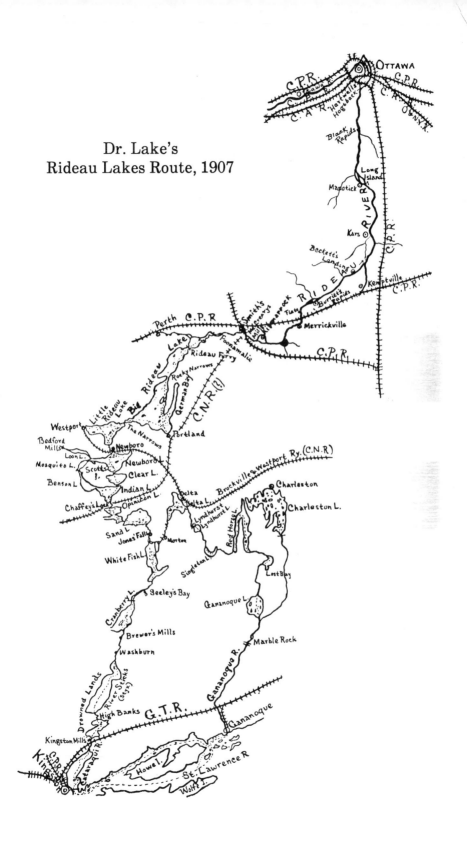

Dr. Lake's
Rideau Lakes Route, 1907

Navigator

For purposes of this book, the navigator is the person in charge of the vessel. A commercial ship's captain is normally not responsible for either its passenger list or its ports of call, but only how to get there safely. Our navigator is responsible for all three.

Operator

The person operating the controls of the vessels, who may or may not be the navigator.

The Rideau

The system's official designation is "Canal". However,this pedantic term calls to mind, as Legget puts it, "the murky industrial trafficway". Waterway and River are therefore used interchangeably with Canal.

PILOT
The Pilot joins a ship to advise the
Captain on the navigation ahead.

INTRODUCTION
Maximizing Productive Time

"...lovers of boat and tent may enjoy to the full the varied beauties of the Rideau Route."
—Dr. E.J. Lake, M.D., C.M., 1907.

Productive time, for the Rideau navigator, is that spent in such rewarding pastimes as dropping the hook beside a good swimming hole for a splash, soaking up some peace and quiet, wetting a line from the dinghy to catch supper, exploring some hidden bay just because it's there, or laying on a few extra knots across the open water to feel the wind.

Unproductive time is that spent searching for a berth as the sun sets all too quickly, drifting off the approach wall ten minutes after last transit, or wondering how a whole shoal managed to grow up since you last passed through and how you can get your prop back in true on a Sunday. Very unproductive time is explaining to the authorities how you lost someone overboard who was not wearing a lifejacket or how that canoe got in your way.

While Rideau navigators come in all shapes and sizes, they tend to fall into two broad categories. The first consider their boat simply as a conveyance, a camper that floats. The second take pride in running a "happy ship", navalese for well found, fitted, crewed, stored and sailed. Their craft take them where and when they want to go in safety and comfort. They "maximize productive time" through good planning and organization.

Like any good sports person or hobbyist, the happy ship sailor is on a permanent learning curve. Learning is part of the fun, not a chore. So even if you have been round the buoys a few times and

9

find a lot of this stuff old hat, you might still find something of interest, or something to argue about, in these pages. For the novice, going out on the water can be about as much fun as you can have with your clothes on, (the two activities are not mutually exclusive), and the more you learn about it, the better it gets. Even if the Rideau is not going to be your cruising ground, there is material in these pages that may help you wherever you plan to sail. In business terms, productive time and production go up, along with customer satisfaction. Knowledge is power, particularly if it helps you avoid making an ass of yourself in front of your crew.

Several people with professional and/or personal marine backgrounds and knowledge of the Waterway have reviewed this text for technical accuracy and concur with it. (See Acknowledgements.) The author sleeps much better knowing that, if errors are to be found, he can share the blame with them. The text was also reviewed by some lay people, who advise that they can actually understand it, so it is O.K. to let minors read the book. I thank them all for their critique, comment and not demanding a share of the royalties.

Purposes Of The Book

A book aims to either enlighten or entertain. This book proposes to tap both markets by enlightening in an entertaining way. It starts with the thesis that boating for pleasure is serious business. With our climate, the job, and other distractions, time available for getting out on the water should not be wasted on unproductive activities. While boating offers much more freedom than driving a car, (what the hell is an "open road" these days?), even the simplest outing requires some preparation. Cruising requires much more, because one is eating and sleeping aboard the boat, or camping out of it, not just navigating the craft. In addition, knowing where you are going and what's along the way will make for a better trip. Ergo, some research is advisable and some documentation is required.

We, (my wife and I - the royal "We" comes with the second book), have buoy-hopped most of the Trent-Severn Waterway without charts or other paper on board, and managed to avoid hitting anything serious. But with our cavalier preparations, we wasted some time. We got turfed off the marine railway for operating an unlicensed boat, lost the channel a few times, and missed some interesting places because we didn't know they were there. Obviously, some reference material would have been useful.

Of course, you can go too far the other way and get swamped with the stuff. What first gave me the idea for this book was the abundance of material available on boating in general and the Rideau Canal in particular. Even living in Ottawa, where the head offices of the four federal agencies, and regional offices of the two provincial agencies involved are located, it took many days to marshal all the material listed in the bibliographies. Even more days were required to find out what was in it.

While the material is all good stuff, I concluded that:

1) Much of the material is duplicated in the many different publications.

2) Much of it is extraneous to the requirements of the Rideau navigator.(E.g., do you know that there is a 9 k.p.h. speed limit on sections of Wascana Lake, Sask.?)

3) With 50 years of messing around in boats, 24 years in the Canadian Coast Guard under my belt, and many friends in the marine community, I should be able to add a few pointers myself.

Purpose 1

To take all this material, boil it down to its essentials and;

■ add some choice morsels from my own and others' experiences,

■ mix in a few witticisms and cute anecdotes to illustrate points and keep the reader awake through the heavier stuff,

■ add bibliographies of related publications for those masochists who really want to get into it,

■ have the thing vetted by qualified people, then polish it into a pretty useful read of manageable size for the Rideau navigator.

The Rideau Navigator is not a stand alone book. Any ship's master worth his/her salt would rather appear on the bridge without pants than without charts (and not a few have). They are considered so essential at sea that it is an offense under the Canada Shipping Act for a ship to navigate without proper charts. Therefore, Rideau Waterway Small Craft Charts 1512 and 1513 are the fundamental tools, not only for the voyage itself, but also for making the voyage plan. The Canadian Hydrographic Service's Small Craft Guide-Rideau Waterway And Ottawa River also provides useful navigational information.

The Rideau Navigator is also not a tourist guide. There are several good ones available and some of the best are listed in the Bibliography of Tourism. See also Chapter One for some more ideas on finding out what to see and do. This book doesn't intend to promote the Rideau, the Waterway certainly doesn't need me for that. My job is simply to advise on how to navigate it.

"How To..." books usually skim over the "How To Get Ready To..." figuring the reader has already done all that. This one starts before the ice is off the water, about the time the spring boat show season starts. That is when the fun should get underway. (If you didn't get this book until later on in the season, you'll just have to read it faster to catch up.) However, when you are starting to think about getting out on the water, bear in mind the words of one long distance racer; "You can get roughly the same thrill simply by standing in a cold shower tearing up fifty dollar bills."

A Decent Boat

Purpose 2

To make the author rich and famous. I reckon that this is the only way I will ever be able to get a decent boat.

The Rideau Charts

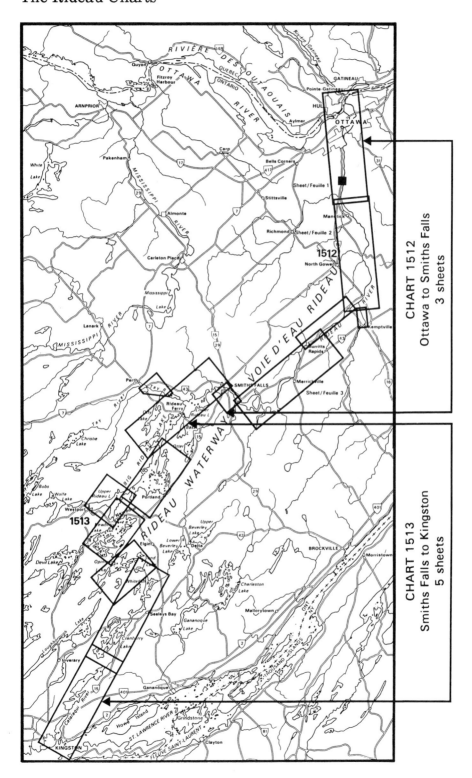

CHART 1512
Ottawa to Smiths Falls
3 sheets

CHART 1513
Smiths Falls to Kingston
5 sheets

CHAPTER I
Warm-up Exercises

"An ideal route for launches and canoes should be strewn with towering rocks, shady nooks, mirrored islands, beautiful bays, narrow passages, varied scenery of lakelet and river with no very great expanse of water where waves may run high; should be plentifully supplied with camping spots; should abound in fish; and should have places scattered along it where all needed supplies may be obtained and where entertainment and shelter at good hotels may be found when desired.

All these and more are found on the "Rideau Lakes Route"; but along the way are scattered many dangers, especially to launches, if the steamer channel is not known and followed."

—Dr. Lake.

Before engaging in any intense activity, the wise planner gets mentally tuned up. The mind must be purged of the winter's carbon, the interest stoked, the itch to be afloat itching. Voyage planning is heady stuff, so shocking the system into gear is to be avoided. The grey matter wants a nudge, not a kick. The following exercises are therefore recommended, not only to get the soul stirring, but also to help get a sense of what lies ahead.

Exercise 1

Lay out the charts and their latest amendments. If your charts are old and worn, they will bring back memories of the great spots you stopped at, where you caught, or lost, the big one, the nice lockie who squeezed you in when you thought you'd have to wait, the places you didn't have time to take in, the ones you want to see again, and the ones you don't. If the charts are fresh out of their plastic, you can have a whole new world to discover.

Charts are made to be studied, not just glanced at. A road map shows you where the roads go, distances, town layouts, and whether the road is paved, gravel, or may be washed out next spring. A chart, on the other hand, shows the topography of the area, above, at, and beneath the water's surface.

Supertug

Above the surface, the dark brown contour lines, with their elevations in feet, describe the terrain. Widely spaced lines mean smooth land with few features. Closely spaced lines indicate steep slopes. If the lines run close to shore, you have a steep, usually rocky shoreline with deep water probably, but not always, running close in. Getting ashore there could be difficult. The charts also show man's contributions: roads, bridges, towns, power lines, and other structures.

At the surface, the charts show marshes and drowned land, rapids, bays, channels, rivers, creeks, and open stretches where one has to mind the weather. Man has added locks, walls, canals, dams, piers, marinas, and other construction. Most important, charts show the aids to navigation (each numbered for identification), and the recommended track.

Beneath the surface, charts show the profile of the bottom by a system of colours and sounding (depth) numbers. A blue background means 1 m (3 ft) or less. Light blue is 1 - 2 m, and white is more than 2 m in depth. The black numbers give depths in feet. This profile tells you where you can or cannot safely navigate, depending on the draught (underwater clearance) of your craft. The soundings, established navigation channels, and the presence of underwater power cables and other obstructions also tell you whether you can anchor at a given spot.

The charts and their jackets provide a wealth of other data, such as:

Chart Datum. This is the minimum controlled water level. The chart soundings are given for this level.

Distance Scales in statute miles and feet. Soundings are also shown in feet. This is important for the metric person. The number "20" in miles equals 32 in kilometres. On the other hand, "3" means lots of water in metric, but not very much in feet. To add to the fun, the speed limits are also in metric. This only sounds confusing because it is. However, Colonel By built in feet, and who are we, mere civilians, to correct him? The key is to always be clear on which system is being used for what, and convert as necessary.

Logarithmic Speed Scale. This is a handy way to calculate your speed over the ground in statute miles per hour. (See Chapter Two, Section 2.)

Profile Of The Waterway. This shows the distances between locks and the height above sea level of each stretch, (for those of you who suffer from altitude sickness).

Chartlets of each lock or set of locks, including their approaches. Note that each chartlet has its own distance scale.

Compass Rose. This gives both true and magnetic north. It is useful for checking your own compass, which shows magnetic north, plus or minus its own deviation. More important, if you can't make out the direction of the channel, the compass rose will help to give you the course.

Relationship Amongst The Features. How the features, above, on, and beneath the surface relate to each other can only properly be displayed in chart form. This form can answer such questions as, how much to the right of is, "a little to the right of", Shadow Rock? Can I get to Barr Island through Bedores Creek with my draught, or do I have to go way around Scott Island? How long will the run take, considering that I have to reduce speed through Elbow Channel? A good navigator can study the chart, check the weather, read the traffic, and come up with a pretty good idea of what conditions lie ahead.

Exercise 2

Browse through the Small Craft Guide. Besides navigational data, it mentions points of scenic and historic interest, boating and tourist facilities, and other general information. The index gives the page numbers where place names may be found in the text. The second edition is current to 1986.

A second book to read for enjoyment and navigational information is Dr. Lake's Chart Of The Rideau Lakes Route, first published in 1907. I have used some of his more delightful passages to lead off these chapters and they may give the impression that this is not a serious work. Not so. Dr. Lake was a keen observer of the Rideau's geography and his descriptions are precise and accurate. After all, Dr. Lake was an "Eye, Ear, Nose, Throat and Skin Blemish Specialist", and if you can't ask one of those for sailing directions, whom can you ask?

Exercise 3

Check in with your tourist bureau. It is a good idea to know what there will be to see and do along the Waterway when you go. While the references in the Bibliography of Tourism are useful, they may not tell you what events and activities will be going on during your cruise. There are probably things that you will want to make, others that you might check out if you have the time, and still others that you would just as soon skip. For instance, if there is to be a Caber Catching Festival at Macgillicuddy's Landing, complete with topless Scottish dancers, are you going to think, "That'll really cap the trip!" or "Who the hell wants to spend all day dodging cabers? Besides, we'd bust our bagpipes trying to find a berth in that lot. We'll give it a miss."

Exercise 4

Visit the Rideau Museum in Smiths Falls. From a strictly navigational point of view, it doesn't have much to add to the charts, but it does give a sense to the Rideau. It shows the system as not just a big ditch for you to run your boat along, but a living, breathing waterway, with a history directly related to the development of our country, a very lively present, and, if we treat it with the respect it deserves, a future just as promising.

C'mon in!

Your cruise will be more enjoyable if you know what is behind the things you see.

Don't be put off by the Park historians' bland language. The Waterway was not built through virgin territory. Other people, with their own way of life, were here before Colonel By. Picture, if you will, some entrepreneur, having sunk his life's savings into grain mills, breweries, and other industries dependent on water flow. Along comes this trumped up limey Colonel, all sword and epaulets, digging this great bloody ditch. Said Colonel then proceeds to tell said entrepreneur that His Majesty now has sole control over the use of the Waterway and its levels, for the Glory Of The Empire. The historians must have pondered deeply on how to phrase the discussions of the time in language suitable for impressionable children.

Exercise 5

Drive the Rideau Valley. Spend a day or two shortly after ice out along the byways. Highways 15, 16, and 43 parallel the Waterway and secondary roads will take you in to the locks. While the system may not yet be filled, you will get a good feel for the country it passes through. Brochures and other materials describing the local tourist sights, boating facilities, coming events and other facts of interest are usually available at hotels, stores, and tourist spots. Marina and gas station operators are often founts of local knowledge, particularly if you show a genuine interest in their area.

Lesson For To-day

1) Study the charts to get a handle on the layout of the Rideau as a whole.

2) Read the Small Craft Guide to see what's in it. For more colour, read also Dr. Lake.

3) Check in with the Tourist Bureau for things to see and do.

4) Visit the Museum to see what the Rideau is all about. If you meet the Colonel's ghost, take it to lunch. If you meet the author of this book, send him home to his mother with a note.

5) Drive the Valley. Get a feel for how the country that you have studied in two dimensions on the charts looks for real in three. In early spring, you risk getting stuck in the mud. That should hurry you into your boat so that you can sail Dr. Lake's "dustless courses of the Rideau."

Now the juices should be flowing and we can start planning the voyage.

CHAPTER TWO
Making The Voyage Plan

"...there is a shallow portion with mud bottom which holds back speed of deep draught boats. This shallow streak ends not far out from the wharf so that a deep draught boat will spring ahead just as it is approaching the dock."

—Dr. Lake

Most voyage plans start at the point where one is, "in all respects, ready for sea". They assume one has already done all the preparations. The plan simply sets out where and when one aims to go. This book starts at the real beginning, where one is "in all respects ready to start planning, not only where and when, but also with who, in what, and how fitted and stored."

If you're the type who simply wanders down to the wharf, starts her up, casts off, and sets off to find out what is going to happen to you, you may not find this book of much interest. My poor starving children thank you for buying it anyway. However, if you're the type who likes to feel that you have something of a handle on things when you leave port, welcome aboard.

1. Bodies And Boats
All kinds of craft go cruising on the River, from 2 m (6 ft) inflatables, canoes, through sailboats, cruisers, and tour boats to specialty craft, and there are pros and cons for each. In a large cruiser with accommodation, one is pretty well self-contained but also limited as to where one can go outside the main channel. In a small craft, one has to come ashore for accommodation, but is free to roam wherever there is some blue on the chart. The only real requirements for a boat to go cruising in are that it float,

Bodies and Boats

move, and be big enough, and safe enough, to carry one's party and stores. We cruise in a 4.5 m (14 ft) car topper. When comparing notes with a large boat owner, I like to conclude by saying, "Let's compromise - your boat and my gas bill."

a) Match-Making. Few of us are in a position to be able to saunter down to the boat house saying something like, "We're off down the Rideau, James. We'll be six, so we'll need the Chris-Craft. Bring her round and gas her up, would you. Then you can finish recalibrating the satellite navigation in the Bertram." We, unfortunately, have to go with the boat we have, or whatever we can charter, borrow, or pirate.

One of the first things one notices about boats is how much they shrink when one goes from the outside to the inside. Furthermore, the inside is cluttered up with all kinds of stuff—engines, fuel tanks, controls, equipment, seats, etc.—that one really cannot do without. Imagine a rainy day, with all your party stuck inside. Then ask yourself, how many of them do you really want to be stuck inside all day with? A second consideration is sleeping arrangements. You may be given to understand that a certain boat sleeps six. But that usually means, as one charterer aptly put it, "they really have to like each other." In other words, if one clears away these, swings that to the side, folds up the other, and pulls down this, one will find 6 more-or-less flat surfaces, barely able to accomodate 6 more-or-less regular size people, more-or-less. If none of these toss around too much, snore too much, or have to find the heads at 0400 hours, one should get through the night, more-or-less. Sleeping on board is an acquired art, usually acquired by a combination of too little sleep the first night out, too much sun during the day, and a couple of industrial strength sundowners in the evening.

For normal people, and there are not too many of us left on the water, the answer is to keep the numbers down. Crowd the day trips, not the cruises.

b) Big Boats. Not wanting to turn all you "Born To Party" types off the River, I have to report some good news. The Rideau can accommodate vessels up to 27.4 m (90 ft) length over all, by 7.8 m (26 ft) in breadth, by 1.2 m (4 ft) draught. There is a minimum available water depth of 1.5 m (5 ft) in a strip 10 m (39 ft) wide down the centre of the channel. If you are navigating with a draught of more than 1.2 m (4 ft), you must contact the Canal Superintendent. If you can afford a yacht that size, you can also afford your own organizer and drop the whole planning bit in his/her lap. This will free your energies for the real issue, THE PARTY, presumably organized around the premise that, at any given time at sea, somewhere around the world, the sun is over the yard arm.

For most of us, lock dimensions present no problem, although sailors of deep keel boats should mind their draught. The Navy has the real concern. Because of the size of its ships, the Navy is the only one of the three services that cannot fire on Parliament, a fact that has probably governed Canada's defense policy for generations. (Colonel By, you may recall, was Army.) The Coast Guard gets its whack because it operates shallow draught ships.

c) Small Crews. Whatever the size of the vessel, a small crew means more space for some of the finer things of life; good food and drink, extra clothes, extra books and games, and souvenirs and other goodies picked up along the way. Fewer people also means less competition for sunning space, the swimming ladder, and comfy spots for curling up with a good book, or something. It also means less time spent in the galley, and doing other chores.

If you are planning to charter, shop around. Can the boat really sleep your party, or just stow it? Sure, you can reduce your share by spreading the charter costs among more people, but the second night out is a little late to find out that you really don't like cruising in a can.

Two couples we met on the Rideau had their own solution. They had each stripped an 9.3 m (28 ft) pontoon boat down to the deck, leaving only the motor wells and control consoles aft. When lashed together, the two hulls provided a clear deck space about 6.3 m (19 ft) by 6 m (18 ft). Imagine the possibilities. Add a boom box, some coolers, some friends, some more friends with more coolers, ... Then, when it's over, simply clear away enough empties to make room for the tents. In sum, crowds taken in reasonable doses can be fun. But after a while, people need their space. Discovering this a few days out may be too late, and you are stuck with the arrangements. A smaller party for a boat of a given size means more space for everybody to bring what they want to bring and do what they what to do without tripping over each other, and less time required for housekeeping. If you can't stretch the boat, try to shrink the crew by cutting the invite list. Those that survive the cut should be invited early so that they can help out with the preparations.

2. Whither

Where a cruise is to start, where it is to finish, and where it goes in between can be critical to its success. If your start and/or finish points are a long way from where you hope to spend most of your time, you can use up a lot of it just in getting there.

a) Starting Point. With a large craft, you may have a long passage to reach your cruising area, so you should aim for early starts and long runs for the first day or two. If your boat is trailable, your starting point can be just about anywhere you want, as there are provincial, municipal, and commercial launching ramps all along the system. You only need someone to drive you out and pick you up. (On our last trip, it was my mother-in-law. Anything is possible.)

b) Finishing Point. The nice thing about trailering is not having to return through old territory. You can be picked up anywhere. For instance, our original voyage plan had us trailering Ottawa-Kingston, cruising Kingston-Ottawa, and recovering at Dow's Lake. When we were limited to a week-end trip, we went back to the charts and worked out a run that could be done in two easy days. You big fellahs have to finish where your boat's gotta be, which is usually all the way back where you started from. So there.

c) Cruising Style. Some parties want to take in as much of the Waterway as their time permits. Their plan can be ambitious, almost the "If this is Merrickville, it must be Thursday" school of travel. Others are in less of a hurry. They operate on the proven theory that waterways don't move around very much, so what they miss this trip will still be around for the next. Then there is the "grasshopper" technique, named after a method of hunting submarines. The hunter sneaks along for a piece, all ears, and then moves out at full bore, "hopping" over to the next stretch, to settle down and listen again. You can do the same thing cruising, hopping from one interesting area to the next.

Those of you who did your homework like Teacher told you to in Chapter One will know that while much of the Rideau is delightfully scenic, there are stretches which are sort of God's gift to the Flat Earth Society, (old By being Army and all), which may not require one's full viewing attention. These stretches make good hopping grounds.

d) Allocation Of Time For The Voyage. 202 km (126 miles) does not sound like much of a trip. You can drive from Ottawa to Kingston in about 2 1/2 hours, non-stop. However, by water, the voyage is not a clear run. There are many locks and other constraints which increase the time required to make the trip.

Rideau Locks' Hours Of Operation. The Fees and Hours of Operation, issued annually, gives the following schedule. The actual times may, however, vary from year to year.

Fri. of Victoria Day Week-end to mid-June.

Mon. to Thurs. 08:30-16:30

Fri. to Sun., holidays 08:30-19:30

Mid-June to Labour Day Mon. 08:30-19:30

That Tues. to the Wed. following Thanksgiving 08:30-16:30

While night navigation between the locks is permitted, there are only a few lighted aids. Therefore, travel after dark is not recommended for those lacking detailed local knowledge.

Lock Transits. Not counting the 8 at the Ottawa River, there are 41 locks shown along the Waterway. However, the combining of locks at Smiths Falls has reduced this to 39 operating locks, an average of one every 5.2 km (3.1 miles). The shortest stretch is Hartwell-Hogs Back, 1.7 km (1.06 miles), and the longest is Long Island-Burritt's Rapids, at 39.5 km (24.7 miles). For planning purposes, assuming no line ups, which is very unlikely, you have to allow thirty minutes for transitting each individual lock, although it can often be done in twenty. Some 19.5 hours, therefore, should be allowed for just locking through the system.

Restricted Speed Zones. Schedule IV, Part III, of the Boating Restriction Regulations made under the Canada Shipping Act, lists twenty-six "Waters On Which Power-Driven Vessels Are Subject To A Maximum Limit. "(Whew!) Six of these have a limit of 12 k.p.h. (8 m.p.h.) and the rest a limit of 9 k.p.h. (6 m.p.h.). Exceeding these limits can lead to possible wallet-busting fines. These "Waters" are supplemented by several zones marked "SLOW", usually narrow bends with restricted sight lines and/or congested traffic. Operators should obey their better instincts on approaching blind corners by reducing speed and keeping well to starboard. Finally, there are the "Watch Your Wake" zones of which more later.

Stopovers. Progress will be further interrupted by whatever pit stops the party makes. These include fuelling, storing, discharging holding tanks and other waste, seeing the sights, stretching the legs, suppressing the mutinies, or simply changing the pace.

Boat Speed. With all these constraints, diversions, and distractions, the reader may well wonder why I bother with this topic, figuring he/she is never going to get sufficient sea room to get up on a plane anyway. However, it is a fact that many navigators, unless they have checked it out or own a reliable speedometer, do not know what speed their boat is actually making at a particular throttle setting in a given condition of load, wind, current and sea. Furthermore, there is speed over the ground, i.e., distance made good over a given time, and speed through the water. If one is in current, speed over the ground is water speed, (as per speedometer) plus or minus current speed. A run at full speed with only the operator on board will not give the same reading

Nosing in

as when the boat is fully crewed and stored for the cruise. The load not only changes the all up weight, but also the draught and trim, giving the boat a different feel, as well as speed. You should at least know what throttle setting will give the speed required for the twenty-six "Waters". Knowing what you are doing at your cruise setting will let you make a more accurate estimated time of arrival (E.T.A.), at your next stop.

Ever mindful of your welfare, the good folks over at the Hydrographic Service have provided a neat little system for obtaining your speed over the ground. On your chart, select a stretch clearly marked by buoys, wharves, points of land, or other features, equal to some simple fraction of a mile. Time a run in each direction and average the times. Then, turn to the Logarithmic Speed Scale found at the top of Charts 1512, Sheet 2, and 1513, Sheet 3, and follow the directions.

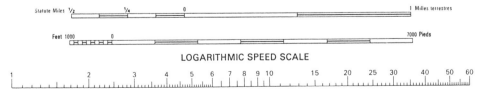

To find speed, place one point of dividers on number of statute miles run and the other on the number of minutes run. Without changing divider spread, place right point on 60 and the left point will indicate speed in statute miles. Example: with 4·0 miles run in 15 minutes, the speed is 16 statute miles per hour.

To get k.p.h., multiply by 1.6. For the "Waters", it takes 10 min. to cover 1 mile at 9 k.p.h. (6 m.p.h.) or 6 min. 40 sec. at 12 k.p.h. (9 m.p.h.).

Where no speed limit, SLOW, or Watch Your Wake signs are posted, you can lay on some speed, commensurate with responsible navigation and good seamanship. However, if your idea of a good boat trip is to really burn up the water, there are far better places to do it than the Rideau, which is, in essence, designed as a cruising ground.

Weather. The reader may think that the following quote from an otherwise forgettable novel about submarine warfare is a bit much for a treatise on navigating a relatively protected waterway. However, it is one of the best descriptions I have come across of how to think of weather at sea. "It, [the sea], is there. It makes its own rules, plays its own game. I mean, shit. Think about it. When a storm hits, the war stops. I mean, that's it. If you are still around when the winds die, you can play some more. But you do it on her terms. You better do it on her terms." In peacetime as well, everything must also stop in order to concentrate on staying afloat and making safe haven.

Sea state, winds, currents, and fog are delaying factors. However, poor weather is relative. A reasonably sized yacht may cruise through a bit of a blow with hardly a bother, while a small craft must proceed with care. Furthermore, the Waterway includes both sheltered channels and open lakes. What is a refreshing breeze on one might be kicking up quite a chop on the other. Even large, well found craft can take damage from a pounding, as well as give a bumpy ride. Finally, no boat is lightning proof.

For small craft, any weather must be taken seriously and for canoeists, it can be critical. Well handled, with strong paddlers, a canoe is an excellent sea boat for its size. However, it lacks the speed to run for shelter and requires continuous physical effort for it to hold a course. A tired paddler can easily miss a stroke, allowing the craft to broach, i.e., swing sideways to the seas. An overturned canoe can be righted, and the crew can climb back in, but it takes a lot of strength and skill.

In essence, therefore, if a navigator is concerned about the weather ahead, he/she should exercise the seaman's ancient prerogative; stay the hell in port. There is no schedule worth going out for, and "Stupid" does not read well on a head stone.

All of the above lecture on navigational constraints being engraved in one's memory by now, one is still left with the burning question, "How bloody long is it going to take me to get my boat down that River?" The answer is six days. That is the time it takes the average navigator, (and you look pretty average to me), to sail the system from one end to the other, in the high season, (July-Aug). It can be covered in less time, but not if you really want to get to know the Waterway. Count on 6 days to do it right. Playing a hunch, the Canadian Parks Service has come up with a Six Day Pass, figuring, with good reason, that you will get so enamoured of the Waterway, you'll want to keep going to the other end. Then they can ding you for another pass to get

home. Since they do about 50,000 lockages a season, putting an average of 3 boats through a lock each time, they have to be on to a good thing. They do their government proud.

But is not progress grand! Six days it now takes. It is said that, in the last century, British troops used to paddle the distance in two days, sun up to sun down. Smart soldiers they. Who wants to hump a load of gear, "Officers For The Use Of", through the bush when it can be floated along?

The Rideau King

Furthermore, in the early part of this century, the steamer Rideau King used to make a scheduled run, Kingston-Ottawa, including lockages and pit stops, in 26 3/4 hours. Now that was steaming! God help any lockie who was slow with his gates when the King was coming through.

Financially, I have to report about the same progress. In those days, passage in the ship was $3 per head. In 1992, the Parks Service was nicking you $26-$103, (depending on boat length), and you had to bring your own ship.

Six days averages out to 33 km (21 miles) per day. This is not a lot, but the idea is to enjoy the trip, not replicate the 24 Hour LeMans', or, come to think of it, your typical crossing in the Titanic.

3. When

The choice of when to go is fairly simple; Spring (Victoria Day-July 1), Summer (July 1-Labour Day), or Fall (Labour Day-Thanksgiving). There are advantages and disadvantages for each season, depending on one's interests.

	SPRING	SUMMER	FALL
Weather	Warm days, cool nights, bugs.	Hot, risk of flash storms, long days, bugs.	Warm days, cool nights
Water Temp.	Cool.	Warm	Cool
Traffic	Medium	Heavy	Light
Hours of Operation	8(11 weekends)	11	8
Queues	Medium	Long	Short
Activities and Events	Some Open	All Open	Few Open

4. The X-Factor

So now you figure you've got it wired, down to the last hour, kilometre, kilo, litre, and loonie. "This cruise, (or this time the cruise), will go like clockwork," say you, "smooth as the south end of a north-bound baby". Well, let me tell you a story.

The Canadian Coast Guard conducts periodic marine oil spill clean-up training exercises in waters across Canada. Part of one exercise, held in the Beaufort Sea, had one of the Coast Guard's fast work boats, (essentially a high speed landing craft), depart from base, proceed along the coast, and recover some equipment for redeployment to another sector. The schedule was tight, but everything, (they thought), had been factored in; weather, tide, ice movement, boat average speed, (both light and loaded), fuel requirements, etc. The schedule could be met.

After a good run out, the craft duly beached, the team went ashore, and load-out of the equipment began. Then the X-Factor, the spanner in the works, crept in. The beach had a very low gradient, and as the equipment came aboard, the draught of the boat increased, cm by cm, slowly putting the boat harder and harder aground, but so gently that the busy team didn't notice. About two hours after beaching, they prepared to depart as planned, just at the top of the tide. But there they were, and there they stayed, watching the tide slowly receding. Their situation report, apparently, was a marvel of creative writing, fair putting to shame my poor efforts in these pages. But the X-Factor, the little thing so obvious that everybody forgets about it until it is too late, never sleeps. Consider it as God's way of keeping us from getting too big for our britches.

5. Do Ya Still Wanna Go?

About this point in the process, the budding navigator has probably arrived at one of two conclusions:

a) Gray has had me working my butt off for a couple of weeks now trying to sort all this out and I haven't even got the damn boat in the water yet. The hell with it. We'll stay alongside all season and party 'till freeze up.

—OR—

b) Ain't that Gray somethin! Got me so exited I'm gonna hock the farm, auction off the kids, and head down the River with the Missus. The way he's got it, this cruisin' stuff's more fun than milkin' Betsy in a blizzard.

If you are of the first persuasion, toughers. This book is not refundable (I hope). If you are of the second, push on. Stamina is a useful trait in this drill.

Lesson For To-day

In making your Voyage Plan, you should have worked out:

1) How many people are going, probably by the simple expedient of cutting your original list in half. Start cutting from the bottom.

2) Where the cruise will start, where it will finish, and how much time you have in between.

3) Based on a rough rate of 33 km (21 miles) per day, where you intend to pass the time. There are lots of ways to spend extra time on the River.

4) What season you are going in.

5) What you want, may want, or won't want to see or do along the way.

6) Some leeway and flexibility built into all aspects of your plan.

We've looked at the vessel, the people and the plan. Now let us see what else has to go into the boat.

CHAPTER THREE
Fitting Out

"It is to be distinctly understood that all three of the above mentioned lights must be kept burning when the vessel is running."

—Dr. Lake

Fitting out is the equipping of a ship, usually a new building or a vessel out of lay up, for service. For our purposes, we will not cover equipment, such as engine controls, which is permanently installed for the craft's operation. Rather, we are talking about the final fittings which will make the craft serviceable.

The equipment and materials to be fitted are discussed in three categories.

1. What the powers-that-be require you to ship,

2. What else you should ship to assist your navigation,

3. What else you should ship to enhance your voyage.

1. Required Equipment And Materials
The Small Vessel Regulations and the Heritage Canal Regulations require that a vessel carry the following:

a) Documentation. License or Registration. Every vessel, "other than one which is not equipped for propulsion by sail or mechanical means" must be licensed, if less than 20 registered tons, or registered, if more. If licensed, its number must be clearly shown. In English, that means, if you drive it or sail it, put a number on it.

Capacity Plate. This plate, usually mounted on or near the transom of outboard powered craft up to 5 m (16 ft) in length, states the maximum power and weight the bare hull is recommended to carry.

Lockage Permit. This is required to transit the locks, but not to navigate outside them.

b) Equipment. The following table sets out the equipment a vessel is required to carry by regulation in accordance with its length.

LENGTH	0-5.5 m 0-16 ft	5.5-8 m 16-24 ft	8-12 m 24-36 ft	12-20 m 36-60 ft
EQUIPMENT				
Lifejacket or P.F.D./person	✔	✔	✔	✔
2 oars & locks or 2 paddles	✔	✔ or anchor on 15 m (50 ft) line		
Bailer or hand pump	✔	✔	both	bilge pump
Fire extinguishers		Note A	Note A	Note B
Flash light or equivalent	✔			
Running lights		✔	✔	✔
Sound device	✔	✔	✔	✔
Flares		Note C	Note D	Note D
Heaving line		✔		
Life ring on 15m (50 ft) line			✔	✔
"Good & sufficient mooring lines"	✔	✔	✔	✔

Note A. 1 Class B-1 if boat has fixed fuel tanks and/or gas or liquid stove or B.B.Q.

Note B. 3 Class B-II + fire pump + 2 pails.

Note C. 3 Type A,B, or C, + 3 A,B,C, or D. Total - 6.

However, vessels in this size range are not required to carry flares if voyaging within 2 km (1 nautical mile) of shore.

Note D. 6 Type A,B, or C, + 6 A,B,C, or D. Total - 12.

Comment

a) Documentation. Licenses and registration are used for identifying boats, particularly by Search And Rescue authorities and Police.

Small craft navigators are advised that it can be difficult for the lockies to read numbers mounted under the flare of your bow. Be prepared to call it up to them if asked.

Capacity Plate. This weight includes the motor, fuel, controls, etc. Thus, in order to calculate the payload (people, equipment, and stores), their weights must be subtracted from the capacity weight. For instance, a 11.5 k.w. (15.5 h.p.) motor, full tank, oars, etc., weigh about 40 kg (90 lbs). My experience has been that, except in fairly calm water, even that payload should be reduced by 10-15%. For instance, in rough weather, I want no more than 3 adults in my boat, which has a capacity weight of 340 kg (750 lbs).

Life Ring

Permit. The fee helps pay the freight, and for what you get, it's a damn good deal.

b) Equipment. Lifejackets and P.F.D.'s must be D.O.T./Coast Guard approved. Our American friends are advised that only the colours red, orange, and yellow are approved in Canada. Jackets must also be properly sized to the wearer. A child size will not support an adult and a child can slip out of, or be suffocated by, an adult size.

Those of us raised in the old kapok "straight jacket" days may have trouble accepting that a modern jacket is a very comfortable garment. In fact, I often wear my P.F.D. as a wind breaker. When properly adjusted, therefore, there is no good reason for people, particularly children and non-swimmers, not to wear them at all times, just like a T-shirt. In a panic situation, they won't do much good stashed under a bunk. In my boat, it's all very democratic. No jacket, no ride.

Anchor. Think of your anchor not just as a parking gear, but also as an emergency brake. If you are moving down on something, and your engine won't stop you, your anchor might. A second anchor can also be useful to reinforce or replace the first. If the anchorage is crowded, a second anchor out the stern will keep your boat from swinging. Be sure, however, to mind the prop. In small craft, the anchor can be used as portable ballast. I can alter the trim of my boat by transferring my 8 kg (20 lb) anchor from one end to the other.

Sound-Making Device. No specific type or decibel level is called for. A handy unit is a small horn mounted on an aerosol-type canister.

Mooring Lines. When locking, you need lines long enough to pass round the holding cables hanging down the walls and back inboard. You must be able to moor either side of the boat. The length of lines should, therefore, be at least twice the boat's beam. If you have stern and/or bow lines on each side, they should be 1 to 1 1/2 times the beam.

We small boat sailors have an additional concern. Approach walls and some Government docks were not designed for us. Their decks are usually higher than our gunwales and their mooring points farther apart than our lengths. We, therefore, need extra long lines to be able to reach those points if we want to tie up both bow and stern.

These lists of required equipment were not put together by some pettifogging clerks in Ottawa with nothing better to do. They were developed by mariners and canal men through years of hard experience. As the equipment's sole purpose is to provide for your safety, I suggest that you use good, serviceable types, rather than the cheapest stuff that will satisfy the law. Using a dollar's worth of frayed line to hold a $60,000 boat makes no sense at all.

2. Recommended Equipment

This list contains everything that I and others can think of that could assist with your navigation. It recognizes that any particular situation may have its own unique requirements as well.

Using a boat hook

Documents. Charts, charts, charts, plus other material as per Section 1.

Fenders. As locks and walls are stone and cement, any damage on contact will be to your boat. However, cheap fenders with weak tie points are not really worth having nor is fendering that does not float. One fender per side is totally inadequate. At least a pair, and preferably more, is recommended.

Extra Line. 30 m (100 ft) of sturdy line will find a multitude of uses. There are better handling types than the inexpensive plastic stuff, such as nylon and polyprop.

Extra Anchor. As in Section 1.

Boat Hook. One or more are useful for grabbing on to things, such as lock holding cables, dock rings, lines, and things in the water. They are also useful for pushing off. A short hook, 2 m (6 ft), is handier and easier to stow than a long one. In addition, extendible models are now available which give the advantages of a short hook and the reach of a long one.

Extension Cord. If all berths or camp sites with power are taken, a 30 m (100 ft) cord will allow you to berth near by and still plug in. If you don't have fitted lighting, an electric lamp is still safer than gas. We use a mechanic's light, which is screened and can be hung anywhere. It should be noted that power is not available at locks.

Binoculars. These are useful for everything, from bird watching, (both kinds), to reading the numbers off buoys, (both kinds), for position checks.

AM and FM Radio. Besides their recreational value, the radio stations provide the weather. Wind strength and direction, and small craft warnings are of particular interest. You, of course, want the local weather. What Ottawa is going to get may not happen in Kingston, so tune into the nearest station, Ottawa, Smiths Falls, Brockville, or Kingston. The news may or may not be of interest. Don't worry if war breaks out. No enemy submarine has been sighted in the Rideau—yet.

Extra Flashlights. Light up your life.

Tool Kit. This should include a good hunting or clasp knife besides the regular tools and tool sets, (wrenches, screw drivers, etc.) The range of tools you take should be governed by your mechanical ability as there is little point in packing tools you don't know how to use.

Spares. A spare propeller, particularly if you have an uncommon size, can be useful. In addition, extra spark plugs, shear and cotter pins, (if your engine uses them), light bulbs, and batteries are worth bringing.

Extra Fuel. If you use a 20 L (5 gal.) day tank, the safest and easiest way to carry extra fuel is in a second tank. It won't bounce around or fall over, and it is much simpler to transfer a hose from one tank to the other than to pour from a gas can. If you don't carry extra fuel, you should top up your tank when convenient, rather than having to go hunt for it when you are getting low. A good rule of thumb is, top up when you are down to half.

Communications. Marine and citizen band radio can be useful if you have them and you can find somebody to talk to. Along with the radio, one needs a license. However, and old sea dogs may weep in their grog when they read this, I believe that a cellular phone will provide a better range of contacts along the Waterway. You can talk to the lockies, marinas, 911, or the local pizza parlour, if you want to. I hasten to admit that this is not a revolutionary idea. The lockies report that every year, more and more boats are coming through carrying phones. I can only hope that, while you're drifting down the Rideau, revelling in the peace and quiet, no telemarketer calls you up wanting to pave your driveway.

Compass. Visibility may become limited through bad weather, darkness, fog, or haze. Then, even a pocket compass, along with the rose on the chart, should help you find your way. However, the compass should be checked for accuracy in the area of the boat where it will be used (to compensate for magnetic interference), before setting out. This can be done by lining it up on a known bearing and checking its deviation.

Electronic Navaids. If you have them fitted, they can be of some use, but they are certainly no substitute for good seamanship. I once visited a neat little 7.5 m (23 ft) cruiser owned by a retired electronics engineer. He had her fitted with all the bells and whistles, albeit more as a hobby than as a requirement. His pièce de resistance was satellite navigation. In theory, he could set it up to take him down the River by itself. In practice, however, there are so many unprogrammable objects, boats, swimmers, dead heads, and the like, on the water, that the system certainly couldn't replace him at the wheel. He also apologized for being unable to give the exact position of our berth. His system worked by triangulating the signals from three satellites and one signal was masked by the tree we were parked under. There could be a lesson for NASA in this. The only aid considered of really practical value is a depth sounder for deep draught boats. In sum, unless your purpose is to dazzle us peasants, a fancy array of electronics is not really required on the Rideau.

Water Purifier. No thanks to us, the Rideau water is no longer fit to drink. Clean water is available along the way, but it requires adequate containers, such as tanks or plastic jerrycans, to carry and store it on board.

Medical. You should carry a good first aid kit complete with splints for fractures, and enough prescription items, including spare eye glasses and other special requirements, to see you through the voyage. It is also useful to have at least one of the crew first aid and C.P.R. trained, preferably the one who is not going to fall overboard.

Comment. There are three things to be noted about the recommended list. All items are potentially useful in minimizing "unproductive" time. The second is that none is particularly bulky and all are easily stowed. The third is none is very expensive. With this endorsement, therefore, you should run, not walk, down to your friendly ship chandler and stock up.

3. Boredom Countermeasures

A couple we know were invited to spend a week-end on the Rideau. "Come along," they were told, "you can sit back, relax, and watch the scenery go by," and that's just what they did. They cast off Saturday morning, got themselves comfortable, and were efficiently chauffeured down the Waterway. They watched the scenery, hour after hour. On Sunday, they were chauffered back through the very same scenery. There was nothing to do on the boat, and the only saving grace was that there were no kids along to be bored as well. It therefore behooves your ship's Director of Recreation and Special Events to lay in some books, games, sporting gear, portable TV or other diversions, depending on space available.

Dinghies. This diversion merits some discussion centred around the question of where in hell do you put one? We are talking here of people-carrying craft, not the little blow-up swimming toys. Stowed on deck, a dinghy takes up a lot of valuable space. Secured on the swimming platform, the most popular system, it is out of the way until you want to go swimming. Davits are better, but much more expensive, and the dinghy is still hanging out over the stern. If you want to put it below, you more or less have to dismantle the thing. Then to use it, you have to bring it up and remantle it. How often are you going to bother with all that? The final option is towing, but you must always keep watch on both the dinghy and its tow line. Furthermore, there may be a lockage charge for towed dinghies over 3.5 m (12 ft) in length. The question really comes down to whether you want to take one at all.

If your modus operandi is to stop over where you can step ashore, then a dinghy is probably more trouble than it's worth, and the lockies and other boaters in the locks will probably thank you silently for not towing one. However, if you like to anchor out, and/or go off exploring, or to wet a line, you may want it along. Your own cruising style should govern your choice.

Towing A Dinghy. When in tow, a dinghy's motor should be tilted up or brought on board and the dinghy's centre of gravity kept aft. If possible, its towing point should be down on its stem, rather than up on its fore deck, to keep the bow up. In open water, the line should be adjusted to allow the bow to ride the crest of a wake wave, not a trough, to prevent sheering from side to side. You should shorten up for close navigation and bring the dinghy right up under your stern for berthing and locking.

Lesson For To-day

In fitting out, you should aim to be:

1) Safe and legal.

2) Reasonably self-contained for navigation.

3) Not bored.

Of course, there is one other thing you should ship which can make up for almost anything you forgot. It's called PLASTIC. Now let's have a look at where you are going to put all this stuff once you have it collected.

CHAPTER FOUR
Stores and Stowage

"Crumbs and a landing net will secure quickly a pan fry of blue sunfish."

—Dr. Lake

1. Stores

A ship's stores are its consumables; food, fuel, sun screen, toilet paper, gin, etc., anything that gets used up. The idea is to carry enough of any particular item to last until it can be replenished, plus a small reserve. It follows that the longer you can go without replenishment, the more independent you are. In addition, to return to an earlier point, the more people you have on board, the more consumables they consume, and the less space you have to carry consumables.

For our purposes, such non-marine items as linen, books, games, and camping gear are lumped under stores. The limiting factor for stores is bulk, not weight. Anything that can be done to reduce bulk, such as concentrates and powders, stripping off excess packaging, reusables, etc., is worth doing if space is tight. The bonus for such tactics is that they also reduce your garbage.

Potable Water. While this can readily be obtained from shore taps and/or your own purifier, it is bulky. It should, therefore, be reserved for drinking, (assuming you drink water), and cooking. Use Rideau water for everything else.

Meals. Since you probably have only limited cooking and cold storage facilities on board, you likely will not have the capability, inclination, or patience for fancy cooking. Meals should be planned with that in mind. If you want a gourmet meal for a change, go ashore and pig out on what's left of your plastic.

2. Stowage

Stowage is the little understood science of packing large amounts of stuff into small spaces in such a way that not only will it stay there intact, but also that you can get at it when you need it. If properly done, it is amazing how much even a small vessel can swallow.

a) Rules of Stowage. Any good bos'n or steward will tell you the five basic rules for stowing stores.

Rule 1. Everything must not only have its place but be secured in it. Otherwise, on hitting your first wave, you will likely find it over the side, all over the deck, or busted. As a corollary, anything taken out, must be immediately restowed after use,

Rule 2. Emergency equipment must be clearly marked and stowed such that it can be brought into use within seconds.

Rule 3. Depending on the locker, you eat either from front to back or top to bottom. Therefore, Tuesday's grub should be stowed behind or below Monday's, not in front or above. You shouldn't have to empty out a whole locker to find one loaf of bread.

Rule 4. Use the equivalent of Harry Belafonte's Tallyman, someone with a list of what is to go aboard to ensure that it actually does so. Now is the time to go back for something, not when you are halfway to Smiths Falls.

Rule 5. Remember that you are stowing consumables. If things seem somewhat cozy at first, you will soon consume your way into more elbow room. You can emulate British submariners in W.W. II. When stowing for a long patrol, they would lay cases of "tinned" goods along the passageways. For the first leg of the patrol, the crew had to move about with a pronounced stoop. As time passed, however, they gradually ate their way down to the deck and could walk erect again.

b) Small Craft Stowage. Small boaters have additional concerns affecting both safety and comfort.

Author and Peg with gear stowed.

Stability and Trim. The transfer of even a small weight about a boat or canoe can affect both stability and trim. Once the equipment, stores and crew are aboard, any list will be readily apparent and must be immediately corrected. An improper trim, i.e., down by the head or stern, may not be as easily perceived. If a canoe is down by the head, she will tend to sheer, rather than track a straight line. If down too much by the stern, the wind will throw the bow around. A motor boat is in optimum trim when the bow wave and stern wake are at their smallest and the bow rises easily to the seas. The trim can be altered by transferring weight, by changing the tilt of the engine if it is an outboard or outdrive, or both.

Weight. Stow the heavy stuff low and the light stuff high.

Spray and Rain. Unlike ordinary water, spray seems to be able to flow uphill, around tight corners, through water-tight seams, and even penetrate sealed plastic. It also slops continuously around the bottom, merrily drowning everything in its path. Too much of it, of course, affects stability, and must be gotten rid of. Even on the calmest day, you are going to have to cross a wake sometime and take spray. Years ago, we had a bow rider out on a Florida waterway; flat calm except for the wakes. My wife complained that I was taking them too fast and bouncing her around. (She doesn't bounce well.) Being a kindly operator at heart, I said nothing and took the next one at a crawl. The crest rose, our bow didn't, and we took it green. Fortunately, however, most of the stuff lying on the floor boards belonged to the wife, not the operator.

Rain doesn't seem able to penetrate as well, but it can still put a damper on things and fill the boat. At any rate, we have to keep trying. Wrap everything you can in pressure tested plastic or steel and leave any valuables that might rust at home.

One final caution. As you cannot move about in a small craft while underway, any equipment or stores you might need must be stowed right at hand. Of course, since you can't stretch your legs or widdle either, you probably won't be at sea all that long anyway.

Lesson For To-day

Assuming you haven't run out of room, you should now have on board;

1) All the equipment you are required to ship, and all you have decided you ought to ship, for safe and proper navigation.

2) Some things to raise the boredom threshold.

3) Sufficient beans, bacon and beer to satisfy the inner man and petrol, oil, and lubricants to satisfy the inner boat.

4) You have it all stowed where it is safe and secure and you can find it without having to take the boat apart. (Yeah, right.)

We are now ready to address the next question, namely, how do we get ourselves and our loved ones down the Waterway in a manner fit to earn a nod of approval from those most discerning of critics, the lockies. They have seen everything come down, so it will take some doing. We will therefore impress the Bejesus out of them through a system called Responsible Navigation.

CHAPTER FIVE

The Responsible Navigator

"The water of this lake is very clear, rivalling the St. Lawrence River as a beverage."

—Dr. Lake

The responsible navigator recognizes that he/she is accountable (in many cases, legally so) for;

1. The safety and welfare of the people on board his/her vessel as well as the vessel itself.
2. The effect of his/her navigation on the safety and welfare of other users of the Waterway, and their property, both afloat and ashore.
3. The effect of his/her navigation on the environmental welfare of the Waterway.

1. The Practice of Safe Boating

a) Unsafe Boating Practices. This is a legal term, covering a multitude of sins, from overloading, to steering too close to other boats and swimmers, impairment, speeding, and many others. In general, if you are doing something which common sense and good judgement say that you ought not to be doing, you are probably practicing unsafe boating. If you are ever in doubt, your friendly Peace Officer will gladly show you the error of your ways, including an explanation of the Criminal Code Of Canada and other legislation and regulation, without even being asked. If you are involved in an accident or dangerous/reckless practices, your not so friendly Peace Officer will....

b) Poor Craft Handling. If a) is caused by carelessness, b) is usually caused by ignorance. In Chapter Seven, you will read about a pair of novices locking through. While I observed this episode, on top of many others, it occurred to me that a crowded lock is a poor place to learn how to handle an expensive boat. This couple should have spent more time on this before they set out. Every boat responds differently to wheel and throttle movements, winds, currents, and other forces. Each has its own stopping distances from various speeds. The navigator/operator should be familiar with all these before setting out. A useful practice is to pick a fixed reference point, such as a buoy with good water around it, and test turning circles, stopping distances, and drift rates and angles, etc., about the point until you are thoroughly familiar with how your craft handles and responds. Then, go alongside a wharf. Put marks on it opposite your bow, stern, and your operator's eye. Then practice going alongside, preferably in differing wind conditions, bringing your craft to a stop exactly opposite the marks and a few cm off the wharf. After you have mastered these operations, you may think about going cruising.

c) Booze. As alcohol is a contributing factor in over 50% of all boating accidents, the Liquor Licensing Act of Ontario is enforced on the water. Alcohol can only be consumed aboard a pleasure craft when it is a "residence". The Ministry of the Solicitor General of Ontario defines that term in its pamphlet Don't turn this into a tragedy...as follows:

" A pleasure boat will be considered a residence only where the following conditions are satisfied:

1. It has the normal amenities associated with a residence (beds, lavatory, cooking facilities);

2. It is not underway, but docked, moored, anchored or hard aground; and

3. It is actually being used as a residence at the time.

The special rules state that no person may operate or have the care or control of a boat which is underway while any liquor is contained in it, except where the liquor

■ is in a container that is unopened and the seal unbroken; or

The Long Arm of the Law

■ is stored in a closed compartment."

"It is an offence for a person to operate, or to have care or control of a vessel whether it is in motion or not while his or her ability to do so is impaired by alcohol or drugs."

This is also an offence under the Criminal Code Of Canada.

d) The Long Arm of the Law. The Law does not ignore you once you are afloat. Peace Officers include all Police and Lock-masters. They have the authority to stop, board and search, and require breathalyzer tests, as well as prevent you from entering a lock, or even navigating at all. If appropriate, they may charge you with;

■ Unsafe boating practices,

■ Alcohol offenses,

■ Incomplete or substandard safety equipment,

■ Being Unlicensed, unregistered, or unpermitted to transit the locks.

You can't escape the eagle eyes of the lockies. They can spot irresponsible navigation from the far end of the approach wall. As they are always talking to each other and to other authorities, if you misbehave at one lock, you may get special attention at the next.

e) Filing a Float Plan. A float plan is a schedule describing where you are going and when you expect to be get there. Rescue agencies, such as the Canadian Coast Guard, like you to file one with somebody who can hold it and contact them if you don't show up. If they know your plan, it helps them to focus their search. However, as often happens, if you later decide to go somewhere else, and don't so advise your plan holder, then your plan is worth diddley squat to the Coast Guard.

A float plan should have a description of your boat, its number, your name, the number in your party and the call sign and phone number of your boat.

2. Respecting Others

Your navigation can impact on other users of the Waterway, without necessarily endangering them.

a)Boat Wake. The wake generated by a boat can travel a long distance, possibly putting at risk any small craft in its way. When the waves hit the shallows, they roll in like surf. If the shore is steep and rocky, they will tend to bounce back on themselves, creating a small maelstrom immediately offshore. This is the zone in which boats are normally docked. Even thick fendering cannot absorb all the shock of a boat being continually thrown against the dock, nor can the mooring lines take all the strain and chafe.

In addition, many cottages have lightly constructed docks, either floating or on posts, which can be hauled out in the fall. These docks help the environment by not impeding the flow of water along the shore. However, they cannot take the pounding that permanent docks can. Therefore, in order to protect shorelines, boats, and docks, the Rideau has a "Watch Your Wake" Program in sensitive stretches. Their signs are on these stretches, and as the next step could be mandatory speed limits, it's in everybody's interest to respect the signs by reducing their wake height to a minimum. The responsible navigator will know the height of the wake the boat is generating at different throttle settings by periodically checking the wake and adjusting it to circumstances.

Planing Hull Wakes. No publication I have seen has addressed the fact that a properly trimmed planing hull creates its flattest wake at high speed. By reducing its speed, the craft will actually increase the height of its wake. In theory, assuming there is plenty of open water to manoeuvre, the kindest thing an operator can do for the neighbours is to maintain his/her speed and keep a good distance away. However such logic is not usually apparent to those neighbours. I have gone by other boats, particularly canoes, at full speed and keeping well clear, with a nice flat wake, and had them shake their fists. I have also gone by them, ostentatiously reducing my speed, (and doubling the height of my wake), to waves of appreciation. I must confess, I don't have the answer. I must also stress that this planing hull business does not apply equally to larger craft. They don't plane efficiently with flat wakes and they certainly aren't as agile around other boats as my 4.5 m car topper. Besides, having one of these things bearing down on you at 25-30 knots will unravel any canoeist, and Joe Leadfoot might have problems explaining his laws of hydrokinetics to the Fuzz. My advice, therefore, is to cool it. You don't get flack for slowing down.

One paramount point. If your wake puts lives at risk, or causes damage to property, there is almost no defense available to you before the law. Somewhere along the Rideau lives a policeman who owns a fairly mean boat. He is rather proud of the beast and doesn't like to see it banged around by thoughtless wake jockeys. Unlike the rest of us, who can only stand on the wharf shaking our fists, he can, and will, do something about it. You are warned.

b) The Uninvited Guest. It is not difficult to make yourself totally obnoxious on the water. Some people seem to have trained for it. If you want to get yourself run off the River, therefore, here are some helpful hints.

Private Docks. Some folks hold that, because private docks and floats are built out over public waters, anybody can use them. While the law may not be 100% clear on this, I suggest that the structure itself is private. So if you tie up to or get out on one, you may well be trespassing. At any rate it is suggested that you don't leave your boat unguarded, or you may have to go swimming for it when you return.

Private Shorelines. Years ago, when the local public required access to the shore line to draw water or get ashore, a piece of the foreshore was kept open for access. Times have changed and this right no longer exists except for emergencies. Once you cross the high water line, you are trespassing.

Other Bothers. You can antagonize your neighbours in many ways. For example there is excessive noise, including machinery, and loud music, especially late at night, invasion of privacy, interference with fishing and swimming, impeding navigation, and blinding people with a spotlight, to name a few. Some of these are chargeable offenses.

Naturally, your neighbours on shore are not without recourse. A friend of mine used to have an irrepressible urge to do some skeet shooting down by the water, when he thought he was being unduly imposed upon. Of course, it was all legally and safely done. The offenders seldom realized that they were the subjects of a well rehearsed routine. It was all very noisy and they could only hope that he was not the excitable type. They usually found it prudent to move on. In essence, therefore, the Golden Rule should be followed—if you do unto others, you may be ducking skeets.

3. Protecting The Marine Environment

a) Waste. If you live aboard, you will have to dispose of garbage, black water (toilet waste), and grey water (sink and washing waste). Under the present Province of Ontario Environmental Protection Act, neither of the first two can be discharged into the environment, and the policy on the third is under development.

Garbage must be brought ashore, preferably bagged, and deposited in proper receptacles. Lock stations and some other receiving facilities have separate containers for bottles and cans.

Black Water holding tanks can be emptied only at registered pump out stations and must be fitted with the pipes or hoses to permit this.

Grey Water. In the spring of 1992, the Ontario Minister of the Environment stated that the present regulations governing grey water discharge would be amended. "Within five years of the proclamation of the amended regulations, new boats constructed or sold in Ontario would be required to have necessary equipment to store grey water on-board for eventual release at properly equipped marinas." What this will mean is a large, probably 150%, increase in the amount of water that must be held and probably more frequent pump outs.

Pumping out

Water Conservation Tactics can reduce the grey water that must be held. Some suggestions are;

■ Using facilities ashore as much as possible. You can wash many things in a washroom besides your hands.

■ Rinsing your dishes, without soap or garbage, in the River, stowing them until after supper, and then doing one wash up.

Considering the present state of the Rideau, I see no reason why we all can't start our own conservation program on our next trip out. In addition, a 20 L (5 gal.) plastic container should hold most of the grey water until you can at least get to the next washroom or other facility hooked up to a sewage system. The next best way is to dump it out well back from the shore. The third best is to dump it over the side. You choose.

Pumping out

Fuel. While raw gas, because it evaporates, is a minor pollutant, oil, including that mixed with gas, is a major one. The Pollution Prevention Regulations prohibit the discharge of oil from a vessel. Don't spill any fuel or lubricants into the water.

Environmentally Friendly Products. The use of such products, whether they are no-phosphate, biodegradable, or conservatively packaged, still creates waste, albeit more friendly waste, and it must be treated as such.

b) *Wake Damage.* Bill Mather makes his living on and around the River as a hunting and fishing guide and trapper out of Chaffeys Locks. He loves both his work and the environment he works in. Because he earns his livelihood from them, he has to

Proper weed control by harvesting.

be concerned with the welfare of the fish, the game, and their habitat. His credo is simple. If they are over-fished, over-hunted, or over-trapped now, his future livelihood is gone. He puts it in terms even a city slicker can understand. "If I shoot a duck, I've killed one bird. If my wake flips over a nest, I've killed a whole family. If it washes out the banks and silts up a marsh, I've wiped out a whole flock because I've destroyed their nesting and feeding grounds." Bill runs the same trap line year after year, so he knows that piece of shore intimately. Each fall, he sees the new damage caused by that season's boats; the overturned nests, the loon nests in particular, the drowned dens, the silted up spawning beds, and the trees felled by the undermined banks. He sees the new weed and algae growth caused in part by the excessive nutrients washed down off the banks by boat wakes.

Shortly after ice-out in the spring of 1992, I walked Kerry's shoreline. Although it was faced with rock, the waves were undermining it and the soil was washing out, threatening to silt up a nearby spawning ground. Kerry, facing an extensive, and expensive, reinforcement project, plus a damaged fish habitat, was not a happy man. Since the land fronts a sheltered channel, the erosion could only have been caused by the wakes of passing yachts. You will never see this as you churn down the channel, but your wake is doing its stuff inshore. Perhaps in a few years, Bill will be on the beach, Kerry's foreshore will be destroyed, the Rideau won't be worth cruising, and the irresponsible navigators will be wondering why. On the other hand, perhaps we will get our act together and the Rideau will still be worth a visit by our kids.

c) Zebra Mussels. These are small, less than 5 cm (2 in.), striped clam-like animals that adhere to any underwater surface, such as hulls and immersed boat trailers, and then proceed to breed like flies. They can be removed by either washing down with a hot solution of soap and bleach or leaving the surface out of the water for a few days. Both should be done well back from the shore. The mussels should be reported to the Ontario Ministry of Natural Resources or the Canadian Parks Service.

4. Stewarding The Ship

Responsible navigation is an awful lot easier in a well stewarded boat. You can find things when you need them, you are not trying to cook breakfast and lock through at the same time, and you're not always tripping over stuff that should have been put away.

For Example: A party rented a medium-sized house boat for a cruise down the Rideau. Since this book had yet to be written, they lacked the benefit of the sage advice in Chapter One, and crowded 7 or 8 people aboard, including small children. They had a ball. Their method was simple. They were organized from the start, they had a leader who knew the cruising game, and the crew were willing to learn. Here is how it worked.

a) Crew Duties. These were allocated and rotated fairly so that no-one felt put upon, and each one was capable of doing his/her tasks. Each was assigned certain things to bring along so that there was no duplication or gaps. On board, safety was practiced as a matter of course, including the idea that every adult was responsible for all the kids, regardless of their ownership.

b) Neatness. It only takes a few minutes to clutter up a crowded quarters, so nothing was left lying around. Anything taken from its place was returned immediately after use. (Kids can learn to put away toys when they discover that's how real seamen do it.) Bunks were folded up first thing in the morning and unneeded clothes stowed. Garbage went straight into the bag and the full bags were secured for disposal ashore. On deck, all lines were coiled and fenders brought in as soon as they had cast off.

c) Cleanliness. Dishes were at least rinsed after each meal, spills were wiped up and table and counter tops wiped down. Decks above and below were swept, (but not holystoned), as required.

d) Hazardous Materials. Their vessel carried engine and stove fuel, cleaning agents, and other substances. They followed the manufacturers' instructions for use and storage, particularly in reference to fire and ventilation. When refueling, they placed their tanks on the dock rather than filling them in the boat.

With all those hands available, the work certainly wasn't onerous. The key was to keep atop of it and not let things build up. The kids, of course, loved being part of the crew and took their sea duties seriously.

Lesson For To-day

Responsible navigation is a serious business, involving lives, expensive property, and the Waterway itself. I have adopted that tone through most of this chapter and I hope that some of it will rub off on you as potential navigator. Your Five Commandments, (mariners only need five-you can't covet much at sea, except your neighbour's boat), are:

- First. Thou shalt safeguard the lives and welfare of the people and vessel in thy charge.

- Second. Thou shalt not put at risk the lives and property of others who share the River and its shores.

- Third. Thou shalt protect what is left of the purity of the waters and the land for those who follow. Thou shalt not hide behind the feckless excuse that thy tiny bit of dirt won't make any difference, knowing full well that it is these tiny bits that collectively are the problem.

- Fourth. Thou shalt remove the hated Zebras from thy hull and trailer.

- Fifth. Thou shalt keep thy flock busy and happy and thy craft a pleasant place.

There. Now prick your finger and make your mark at the bottom of the page.

Consider yourself as having achieved the correct frame of mind to navigate the Rideau in a fit and proper manner, a credit to your breed. Next, we will look at the navigation system, which the good folks who run the Canal have laid on to keep us out of trouble.

CHAPTER SIX
Navigating the Rideau

"If, then, when the bow is pointed straight at the one and the stern is not exactly directed towards the other, turn the boat for a little while towards the side to which the stern should go and then head on the bow point again and see if the stern is right yet, and so on till you have it exactly."

—Dr. Lake

Navigating the Rideau is not all that difficult. The main track is well marked, and you are almost always either within sight of a buoy or day beacon or in a narrow channel with only one way to go. As all the aids are numbered, with the red buoys having even numbers and the green ones odd, you can check their numbers against those on your chart and that will locate you exactly. Once you leave the marked channels, however, you either have to navigate by the soundings on your charts, or have extensive local knowledge.

Unlike reefs in the South Seas, shallow water in the Rideau seldom announces itself by a change in colour or breaking swells. It is more likely that the first indication you will get that you are in shoal water will be some very expensive sounding noises from below. When we run the shoals, my wife gets up in the bow, looking down, and slightly ahead, guiding me with hand signals. I slow to a crawl, and when she shouts, slap it into neutral, so that, if we strike, there is no damage. Of course, we only draw about 50 cm (18 in.), and if necessary, we tilt up the motor and row. Somehow, I doubt that this form of navigation would work in a cruiser. A further point is that soundings cannot guarantee that no logs or dead heads have drifted into the shallows.

1. Aids To Navigation System (Navaids)

The navaids system is fairly basic by deep sea standards, but certainly more than adequate for an inland, pleasure craft waterway and daylight navigation. You don't, therefore, have to concern yourself about what to do if you meet up with a slow sweep Racon, or cycle selection errors in your Loran C, or even know how to shoot the sun with sextant and sand glass.

The system consists of fixed, (shore mounted day beacons and signs), and floating aids (buoys). What they are basically saying to you is; "Here lies danger. Pass to port or starboard, as indicated". In addition, there are speed limit signs (buoys with large numbers and pointers,) which give you the allowed speed (in k.p.h.) and direction, and "SLOW" and "Watch Your Wake" signs. Finally, there are a few private buoys, used mainly to mark the entrances to marinas and other private facilities.

Unfortunately, the Rideau lacks some of the more interesting buoys, such as those marking firing ranges, wrecks, munition dumping grounds, isolated dangers and ocean data acquisition systems. Obviously, a low budget operation.

a) The Predominant Colours, Red and Green. The International Association of Light House Authorities has established the Maritime Buoyage System. After, no doubt, much introspection and analysis of alternatives, it has divided the world into two Regions, imaginatively called Region A and Region B. If one is navigating Region A, the red buoys are one side. If one is in B, they are on the other. (I don't know why either.) Canada is in Region B, so the Canadian Aids to Navigation System has our red buoys on the other side, leaving this side for the green buoys. Clear on that?

The I.A.L.H.A. has further decreed that all the world's waters must have up and down streams, whether they want to or not. The Rideau, being a cut above the rest, has two of each, with the town of Newboro having the honour of being at the headwaters of both. What this means is that, as you travel up to Newboro, from either direction, all the aids whose predominant colour is red, must be kept on your starboard hand, i.e., on your right.

(Red is right, right?) These include both red lateral buoys and predominantly red (centre and border), day beacons. Predominantly green navaids must be kept on your port hand i.e., on your left. At Newboro, you go over the hill and start down stream. Therefore, red must now be kept to port and green to starboard. Confused? This may explain why the good folks of Newboro prefer to get around by car.

There are also 5 bifurcation buoys. These indicate to the upstream traveller that the channel bifurs.., bifurcs.., bifurcates.., forks. The buoy has a predominant colour, e.g. red, with a wide horizonal band of the other colour, e.g. green. The predominant colour indicates the main, or preferred, channel, with the other being secondary. The guide is not very helpful for the downstream traveller, so I assume that he/she should treat the buoy as being of its predominant colour. I also suggest that both upstream and downstream travellers should check the chart to see where each channel leads. Who knows? There may be more action along the secondary channel. So when you come up on a bifurcation buoy, just think, your choice may tell the whole world what kind of person you really are.

b) Lights. The Rideau is not totally unsophisticated. There are three lighted buoys on Big Rideau Lake. I am sure there is a good seaman-like reason for lighting up that one section of the Waterway, but it is more fun to speculate on what goes on after dark in the Big Rideau that doesn't go on anywhere else. It should add a bit to your trip. There are also two bridge lights down at Kingston, but we all know what goes on there, don't we.

2. Water Depth

The soundings (depths) on the charts are based on the chart datum, the lowest water level as set and controlled by the Rideau Canal. It will be noted that there is an available water depth of 1.5 m (5 ft) in a 10 m (39 ft) wide strip down the centre of the channel. Unless there has been a very wet or very dry season, these soundings are accurate. Normally, they are regulated so that the variation from datum is less than 2 cm (1 in.). The depths are, of course, in feet.

NAVAIDS

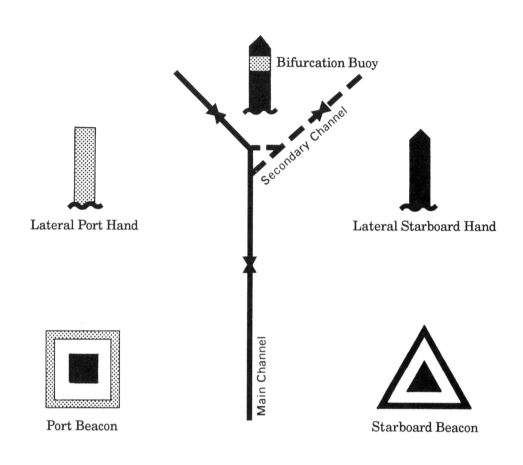

Bifurcation Buoy

Secondary Channel

Main Channel

Lateral Port Hand

Lateral Starboard Hand

Port Beacon

Starboard Beacon

Speed Control Signs

Directional Speed

Regular Speed

Watch Your Wake

It's nice to have your own tug along.

3. The Channel

The channel is for navigation, not parking. That means no anchoring, fishing, or drifting, unless it is an emergency. It definitely means no using buoys or other navaids as mooring posts. If you want to stop, therefore, you should leave the channel.

In sum, one really doesn't require a Certificate of Pilotage to navigate the Rideau. One just stays in the marked channels, works from the charts, uses the compass when required and if available, and respects all speed, SLOW, and Watch Your Wake signs. If one leaves the channel, there are really only the charted soundings and/or local knowledge for finding safe water.

Having said all that, I am constantly amazed at the navigational situations people get themselves into. My latest incident is the large rental houseboat which I spent a good hour guiding out of a swamp. How he fetched up in there would probably make a great story. However, the look on the navigator's face told me it would have been impolitic to ask.

4. Overnighting

There are many ways to overnight. Berths can be found at lock stations, Government wharves, marinas, and commercial docks. Most charge fees of some sort. They may, or may not, have power, and there may, or may not, be fuel and supplies available nearby.

Anchorages are located along the way, and the better ones are so designated on the charts. If you are planning to anchor for the night, look for an adequate depth of water, and shelter, not only from to-day's weather, but also from tomorrow's.

There are public and private camp sites, as well as camping on unposted and/or isolated shores, but watch the fires.

The cardinal rule for overnighting is to have a spot picked out in advance, rather than blundering around trying to find some place at the end of the day, particularly in the high season.

Lesson For To-day

Navigating the Rideau is certainly no more difficult than driving an unknown city street, where you simply stay on the pavement and follow your map and the signs. Moreover, in a boat, you can usually take your eyes off the track once in a while to enjoy the scenery and plan your stop for the night. You won't get swamped in a car, but you will seldom get jammed in traffic in a boat. Your charts will take you down the River, not up the creek.

The most complex part of navigating the Rideau is locking through, and an understanding of that system can do much to simplify the operation. That's next.

CHAPTER SEVEN
Locking Through

"Look out for squirts of water from between the stones as the water drops in the lock."

—Dr. Lake

What sets the Rideau navigator apart from the ordinary boater is the locks, all 47 of them, if one counts the Ottawa River flight. A good lockage is the result of teamwork amongst the lockies, the navigator, and his/her crew.

1. The Lockies
The term "lockie" is designed to show that there are real nice people behind those Lockmaster and Canalman uniforms. However, one Canalman doesn't like my term. Says it is too close to "lackey". That man has a future in this outfit. Did you ever watch a lockie really working the boats on a busy day? It's like watching a good orchestra with the lockie as conductor. Before the music starts, he/she checks out the action on the blue section of the approach wall. A good lockie can call the dimensions of each boat within a few centimetres. The music starts as the gates open. Queue the rental houseboat, because no other boater who knows anything about it will go in ahead of one. Also, the gates are tough, certainly tougher than any boat the rental might run into.

As an aside, we once had the dubious thrill of being in ahead of a rental. One blustery Sunday afternoon, we were properly parked at the head of the lock, all 4.5 m of us, when just before the gates closed, this 13 m (40 ft) monster comes in, sideways. Fortunately for us, the lockie quickly brought her to heel with his boat hook.

It certainly focuses the mind when there is absolutely no place to hide. With their huge boxes of cabins, these houseboats are the playthings of every wind that blows, and their pontoons don't grab enough water to help them hold a steady course. In addition, because they are rentals, it is unlikely that their people have had much time to learn all their quirks.

Meanwhile, back with the lockie. He/she continues to load the lock, rafting the boats three across, if necessary. This is where knowledge of dimensions comes in, as the lock may end up wall-to-wall boats. Then the crab is cranked or the button pushed, the gates are closed, and the ride begins. When exiting, the boats are signalled out as if a procession was being formed. The lockies are good, and it is worth remembering that their polite suggestions have authority behind them. Watch and listen for their instructions, respond smoothly, and everything is cool.

2. The Navigator/Operator and Crew

Locking Through Safely suggests that, "Your crew, (adults if possible), should be posted at bow and stern". Assuming the navigator is also an adult, that makes three on board. However, my surveys point out that probably less than half the boats can boast of three adults. More often, it is usually 2 adults, or 2 plus 1 or more children. This means that the operator must either take one line him/herself, after positioning the boat and shutting down, or being prepared to assist a child.

This raises the question of posting the other adult line handler. Three factors should govern this choice;

1. You can swing the stern with your engine, but not the bow.

2. Which end is most readily accessible to the operator?

3. Which is the up wind end? If that end is moored first and released last, the wind will help hold the craft against the wall. If the down wind end is moored first, the up wind end will be blown off the wall.

The other adult should usually, therefore, be posted at the end which will be secured first.

3. Locking Procedures

a) Winds. The wind does funny things around locks and their approaches. No matter how constant it was in the open, it bounces

Turbulence

around the lock areas. You must, therefore, be prepared to correct for gusts coming from any direction.

b) Approach. When approaching a lock area, the operator reduces to the posted speed, watches the wake, and stays clear of boats exiting the lock. If things are quiet, the lockies may be busy on chores. Then, three toots requests them to open one gate, and four requests both. The holding area for boats awaiting lockage is that length of the wall or wharf painted blue. The rule is, if you plan to lock through immediately, tie up to the blue, unless the lockie waves you right in. Moor as far forward as possible, to leave room for those coming behind. It is usually a good idea to let the big boats have the inside berths, so they won't squash the little boats. If you are not going through, you should tie up elsewhere. If you want to stop over, it is better to go through first, and lay over on the other side. That way, you are free to move on whenever you want. This decision should be tempered by whether that side is already full and/or exposed to the weather.

c) Turbulence. Turbulence, ranging from minor ripples to currents strong enough to move a large boat around is found at any lock, both;

- below the lower lock gate when the lock chamber is being emptied, and,
- within the chamber as it is being filled.

Entering with fenders deployed.

If your boat is in either area at the time, it should be secured at both ends. If you are underway, be prepared to respond to the turbulence.

d) Locking. Before entering, all open flames, including smokes, pilot lights, and cooking facilities, must be extinguished, fenders deployed, and lines made ready and free. Bear in mind that the lockie may instruct you to secure either port or starboard side to the wall or to another boat. If not, you should move as far ahead as possible. The operator should bring the craft to a complete stop alongside the black holding cables and about 15 cm (6 in.) off the wall, allowing for his/her anchor platform, bow sprit, swim ladder, and other protrusions. The line handlers then quickly pass the lines around the cables, which hang loosely down the wall, and back in board, where they are held, not tied, and never left unattended. If, as usual, the bow is secured first, enough slack must be left in its line to allow the stern to be brought in. Once safely secured, operator and crew should shut down everything but the bilge blowers, which must be left in operation, tend the lines so they don't get hung up, and stay alert. Not every boater in the lock is as competent as you, and you have no room to get clear if something happens. For example, I watched one yacht, with a crew obviously new on the

Wall-to-wall boats

job, enter a fairly crowded lock. The boat had its anchor catted on its platform in such a way that the sharp end of the base pointed straight ahead, reminding me somewhat of a loaded harpoon. They fetched up close astern of another yacht with an inflatable dinghy lashed on to its swimming platform. I, the lockies and the dinghy's owner silently waited for a surge, a fumbled line, or an act of God to let the point of the "harpoon" close those few centimetres between it and the fully inflated dinghy. I was in a typical writer's quandary; should I write up an exploding dinghy in a lock for this section, or save it for Chapter Eight?

Another insightful aside: I have heard it said that the line handlers should be prepared to take the way off the vessel. I suspect this is a hold-over from the days of 100 kg (240 lb) barge men who liked to pick their teeth with crow bars. I recall watching a 40 kg (100 lb) wife and her young 20 kg daughter trying to stop a 3 ton yacht. Himself (yes ladies, it is always Himself on these occasions) sat at the controls with a zillion horses at his fingertips, wondering what was taking so long. It was a question of which was going to happen first; the boat stops or the girls get dragged into the drink. Remember also, the walls are rough stone and cement, very hard on the knuckles. Himself did not have a very happy crew that day.

e) Exiting. To exit, wait until the gates open or the lockie signals before starting your engine, and make sure it is idling nicely before casting off. On your turn, push off and proceed slowly, recovering and stowing lines and fenders as you move out. Piece of cake.

f) Swing Bridges. If your height requires that the bridge be opened, sound three toots if the lockies have not started to swing it. Wait until it is fully open, and the green light, if there is one, is on before proceeding. Do not impede the passage of other boats, particularly those down bound.

A good crew is a pleasure to watch. Each member not only knows his/her own job, but works with the others. Smart crews wear soft shoes for a good grip on deck. The operation is always done quietly with no roar of engines or shouted orders. The boat eases into her berth as if on rails, the lines slide around the cables and back in a trice, and there is hardly a ripple off the hull. On exit, a slight shove on the wall moves the bow out as the throttle is eased ahead, and lines and fenders are quickly secured. Poetry in motion.

4. Awaiting Your Turn

I have left this to last in order to tell you a story. On a busy day, you could wait your turn to lock through for quite some time and it's not exactly the most exciting occupation going. If one is canoeing, of course, one simply tosses one's craft on one's shoulders, and with a polite sneer for the rest of us crowded into the approaches, lopes easily along the walkway to the other side of the locks, and paddles merrily on. Meanwhile, those in the queue have to keep enough crew on stand-by to take her through when called. If you have a smallish craft, the lockie might let you jump the queue if he/she has a bit of the hole left over that you can be tucked into. So, what's to do to pass the time?

Two retired couples, originally from Newfoundland, were taking a leisurely run along the Rideau for a few days. Since their previous cruising grounds had been the North Atlantic, they hardly felt challenged by the river. As they eased into the crowded approaches to one lock, they realized that they were in for a wait.

A tot and lunch passed the first hour but the line was still moving slowly. Now we all know that making music comes with weaning for Outport Newfies. Without further ado, the two gentlemen outs with their accordion and mouth organ and soon had the joint jumping with some real down home music. The ladies joined in with a few high stepping jigs, to much enthusiastic applause from the other boats. Then, when the Newfies' turn came to lock, they played themselves in with gusto, and the sounds of "The Kelligrews Soiree", or some such, echoed marvelously off the lock walls.

Of course, there had to be a sequel. On their return, several days later, the crowds had gone, and they tied up to the blue alone, awaiting the lockies' call. Nothing. Figuring the lockies had stopped for a cuppa, and being kindly folks, they settled in. However, they realized time was getting on, so they gave 3 polite toots on the horn, as per regulations. Still nothing. Then 3 more toots brought a uniformed head peeking around the corner. A gasp of recognition, and the plaintive cry, "Ohhh Gawwd! Its those crazy Newfies again!" rolled down the channel. Fame is not necessarily a fleeting thing.

Lesson For To-day

1) Mind the other traffic, and respond to fickle winds and currents.

2) Make your movements smooth and easy, both in the approaches and the locks. Let your engine do the hauling, not the crew.

3) Follow the lockies' instructions. They have your interests at heart and will put you right.

4) Have all your fires out and your lines and fenders ready before entering. Stop everything except bilge blowers when secure.

5) Post your crew according to numbers, sizes, winds and which end the operator can manage best.

6) Bring music.

In spite of seven chapters worth of diligent preparation, conscientious navigation, and really smooth locking, emergencies can happen, and the navigator and crew must be prepared to deal with them. Good seamanship is being able to take the "danger" out of dangerous situations. Poor seamanship is making bad situations worse. Chapter Eight, therefore, advises on aspects of good seamanship in emergencies.

CHAPTER EIGHT
Emergencies

"This little book was not published for reference to show you AFTERWARD how you went astray and broke a wheel or put a hole in your boat..."

—Dr. Lake

In this book, an emergency is more than just an inconvenience. It is a situation where lives and/or material could be at risk. However, most emergencies can be resolved, and the situation returned somewhere to near normal. A tragedy, on the other hand, is where losses occur which cannot be restored.

1. Principles of Emergency Response

Resolving any problem requires assessment, planning, and action. An emergency is a problem wherein the success of the response is much more time-critical, and there may be no second chance. The following principles govern the success of emergency responses:

a) Preparation. Ensure that the emergency equipment is on board and working, and the crew knows how to use it. For instance, precious seconds can be saved if people are already in their life jackets and don't have to put them on, (assuming they can). Fire extinguishers are worse than useless if they don't work or the crew can't use them. Repeating to yourself every morning, "It will never happen to me," is not considered adequate preparation.

b) Unity Of Command. Emergency responses cannot be run by committees. Only one person, presumably the navigator, must issue the orders. The others carry them out and advise, as appropriate.

c) Focus. Focus the response first on the lives at risk, and second on material at risk, not on extraneous considerations and distractions. After lives and material are saved, you can see what else has to be done.

d) Stabilization. Take action to prevent the situation from deteriorating further. It may well be all you can do until help arrives.

e) Assistance. If you wait until you are sure you require help, it may be too late to call. By then, your communications may be gone. At least advise potential helpers of your situation and location, even if you don't need them immediately. You can, and should, however, call back after the dust settles and thank them for standing by.

f) Fall Back Plan. If your response could fail, you should have a Plan B. For instance, Plan A could be how to stop the boat from sinking. Plan B comes into force if it sinks anyway.

2. *Types of Emergencies and Responses To Them*

It never ceases to amaze me what kind of pickles boaters manage to get themselves into. The mariner's term for a vessel in a pickle is "casualty". Starting from most severe to least, here are some examples of casualties and their consequences.

a) Violent Destruction of the vessel causing death and injury. This is usually the result of explosion and/or fire aboard. The survivors generally wind up in the water with no resources other than life jackets to assist them. Should the casualty occur in a crowded lock, the impact of the explosion is magnified. Other boats may be struck, and the surviving craft, containing fuel and other combustibles, cannot get clear. Furthermore, the lock prevents the force of the explosion from dissipating. While a fibreglass boat can burn completely out in about 2 minutes, it takes at least 5 to fill or empty the lock and open the gates. There are, therefore, 3 long minutes in that schedule that could get very interesting. This explains why the lockies are such fervent members of the anti-smoking lobby.

If possible, survivors should follow the directions of the lock staff. These may include using the extinguishers they provide and the escape ladders at each end of the lock. Otherwise, about the best they can hope to do is look after each other until help arrives.

In the water, if you can't be rescued immediately, it is best to huddle together to share body heat, flotation, and morale.

b) *Sinking or Swamping.* Again, life jackets are probably your only resource until help arrives. Huddle and hope.

c) *Collision.* This may or may not be serious, depending on the force and location of the impact. There may be death and/or injury and one or both craft lost. If one or both stay afloat, they can at least provide additional flotation.

d) *Person Overboard.* If he/she is wearing a life jacket or P.F.D., recovery is usually simple. Throw him/her a line or life ring. However, if they are not, get to them very quickly and hope they are at least afloat.

e) *Injury.* People can get hurt in boats from a variety of causes. (Lightning, for instance, can cause severe burns, trauma or worse.) If you can at least start treatment, it would help. If you have communications, you may be able to get medical advice, or at least locate and call for the nearest assistance. In any case, travel towards assistance, not away from it.

f) *Grounding.* Depending on impact, and whether the hull is pierced, the vessel can usually be salvaged. We small craft operators do it by stepping out and pushing her off. Larger craft, unless they are well equipped with pushers, may require assistance. It is important, however, to first ascertain whether the casualty is taking water, at least in such quantities that it cannot be controlled. If so, consider leaving her aground for the time being to prevent her sinking. The prop and rudder should also be checked, if only by starting off slowly. If either is bent or broken, they could cause further damage to the boat if you proceed.

g) *Mechanical Problems.* Many mechanical, electrical, or other technical problems can be fixed without professional help. However, even if you have the expertise and equipment on board to make repairs, it takes time. You should, therefore;

- Watch The Weather. It may start off calm, but a rising wind will cause the seas to build and may drift you into danger.
- Get At Least To The Edge Of The Channel. A collision could make you drop your wrench.
- Stabilize The Craft. A steady hull is much easier to work in than one being tossed around. If you can get into sheltered water and/or a wharf, you will have a better platform. Otherwise, you can dampen roll by pointing your bow into the wind by steering into it, anchoring, or tying up to something. If there is nothing else, a buoy may have to do. (Forgive me, Canal people.)
- Get Into Shallow Water to work on the hull or lower unit. You are more stable standing on the bottom and both hands are free.

3. Summoning Help

a) Communications. It is one thing to have communications, telephone and/or radio, and another to know who to call and what to tell them. Just grabbing the mike and screaming HAALP! to the world is not going to do it.

The Message. There are seven things that the recipient has to have:

- name and description of casualty,
- position,
- description of the emergency,
- assistance required,
- number of people involved and injuries,
- immediate situation, and
- your name, phone number, and/or call sign.

The Addressee. A phone or radio operator is essentially a communications link, who may or may not know to whom your message should be relayed. You require that it be passed to an emergency response organization who will know what action to take. Such an organization should be staffed on a 24 hour, 7 day a week (24/7) basis. In order to keep the list short, (so that you can tape it to your set), the following are suggested.

- Telephone-Within Ottawa and Kingston coverage, 911.
Trenton Rescue Coordination Centre
1-800-267-7270.
The nearest Police, via operator.

- Marine Radio-The Canadian Coast Guard guards Channel 16 (156.8 MHz) on a 24/7 basis for distress calls. The Citizen Band Emergency Channel is 9. The Coast Guard does not monitor C.B., but several police and other operators do. For emergencies of "grave and imminent danger", repeat MAYDAY three times. (Mayday is a legally defined signal which must not be abused.) For lesser emergencies requiring assistance, repeat PAN PAN three times. The MAYDAY or PAN PAN alarm is then followed by the message.

Radio operators are advised that, under certain conditions, dead spots occur along the Rideau. You may be heard by other boats, but not by the authorities.

Of course, if all that doesn't get you through, try going ashore, knocking on a door, and asking to use the phone.

b) Audio And Visual Signals. People in the water, an overturned hull, or smoke and flames are obviously the clearest signs of distress, but even they haven't always drawn the necessary attention. Two friends took a canoe out in Mooneys Bay and dumped. It was a hot spring day, but the water was still freezing. Hypothermia was a possibility. Many boats passed by, some even gave a friendly wave, but it took 20 minutes for someone to actually realize that they were in serious trouble and go fish them out.

Officially, you can use;

- flares
- any type of ball shape over or under any flag or square cloth
- sound and/or flash S.O.S. (3 short, 3 long, 3 short)
- repeatedly raise and lower your extended arms (slow flapping)

For my money, you would likely get just as good result waving a towel or cloth, preferably tied to a stick.

Probably the most effective non-regulation signal I've come across was used by a British freighter in W.W. 1. She had struck a mine and just managed to beach to keep from sinking. It was dark and storming, but there was a lighthouse nearby. However, flares, sirens, and whistles would not raise the keepers, so she opened fire on them with her 3 pounder. The keepers were raised.

4. Assisting Vessels In Distress

Many people do not realize that, if they can assist a casualty without endangering their own craft, it is their duty to do so under the Canada Shipping Act. However, this duty extends only to rescuing the people on board, not salvaging the casualty itself. Personally, there is a certain amount of self-interest involved, as well as duty. Every time I give someone else a hand, I am putting out a marker, and the more people on the water who owe me, the safer I feel. Should I get into difficulty, I have markers to call in. This system has a long and honourable history with seafarers.

Following are some practical considerations in rescue work.

a) Approaching A Distress Scene. Wind strength and direction are factors. You have to count on doing some fancy ship handling and your crew may be working over the side. It is wise, therefore, to have any crew that still haven't done so after almost 8 chapters of hectoring about it, put on lifejackets.

People in the water, the casualty and your craft each drift at different rates and angles off the wind. Since you don't want to hit, drift over, or slice anybody with your prop, your safest approach is from leeward, (down wind), and proceeding slowly into the wind.

b) Recovering People From The Water. If they are near your stern, you must put your engine into neutral or shut it off. I prefer the former because I may need torque in a hurry, and that will be just the time my engine decides not to start.

If you toss them a life ring or heaving line, it not only saves them swimming to your boat, but also gives them something solid to hang on to. People can climb aboard much easier if they can use their legs. If you have a ladder, good. Otherwise, make a bight or loop in a line such that it hangs down in the water with both ends tied on deck. If you are in a small craft, be sure to counter-balance the weight of people coming in over the side.

c) Taking People Off A Casualty. The casualty will probably be lying across the wind. If you approach from leeward, you can hook on bow to bow, and she will swing against your side. By keeping the heads of both craft into the wind, roll will be dampened and both craft will be pitching together.

d) Towing. You should approach the casualty's bow from leeward, passing or taking the tow line as you cross it. Before you take the strain, you want the line secured firmly to strong points on both craft, the casualty's outboard or outdrive tilted up, or her rudder amidships, and the bulk of her weight aft. It is recommended that, for a long tow, you proceed first to the nearest shelter, where you can get the tow properly organized. You may want to adjust the tow line, take some of the casualty's people aboard your craft, and transfer some fuel as well, if you are low.

e) Escorting. A casualty usually wants escort when she is not sure she can make her destination. Normally, it is best to escort from astern, where you can keep an eye on her, and she won't be bothered by your wake. However, I once escorted a Coast Guard work boat with engine problems. Her twin diesels left a trail of thick black smoke in her wake which stunk up a good stretch of the St. Lawrence, including my piece, until I moved out on her beam. Every good scheme has its variations.

In sum, besides the safety of your own vessel, your duty ends with getting the casualty's people into safe haven. If the casualty wants a tow back to his wharf, 10 km down the lake, it is entirely up to your good graces whether you oblige or not.

Lesson For To-Day

1) Be prepared in both equipment and outlook. The "can't happen to me" syndrome won't be much help when it does happen.

2) A ship can only have one captain. There is no time to take a vote.

3) Focus your first response on your first priority, the safety and rescue of people.

4) Don't be afraid to call early for help, while you can. Contact an organization that knows what to do and provide them with a clear report.

5) Have a Plan B.

6) If you go to help another, your responsibility is first for your own people, then for the casualty's. You are not obliged to provide free salvage, but it's a great way to make new friends.

If this chapter has taken all the fun out of it, worry not. You could be spending your vacation driving Highway 401. There now, doesn't that make you feel better already?

Now, let's look over some of the boats you might come across in and around the Waterway and then see who, and what, makes the Waterway tick.

INTERLUDE

"All kinds of craft go cruising on the River"

CHAPTER NINE
Keeping The Waterway

"...There is a bush in a stump close to channel, a barrel on a float on the west side of entrance, and a monument-shaped floating buoy on the east side."

—Dr. Lake

I spent, or misspent, my formative summers on the Trent-Severn Waterway at my parents' cottage, which could only be reached by boat. Each spring, on our first run of the season, there were the same buoys, beacons and signs in exactly the same positions they had always been, as though winter storms, ice flows, and other hazards had never happened. Not only were they still there, but they each sported a shiny coat of fresh paint. I don't know why, but in all those years of running that river, I never asked how those aids not only got there, but also kept themselves in such good shape. They could have simply grown up from the bottom, for all I knew. Of course, I also learned that you didn't have to stick to the buoyed channel, there were short cuts. You could get by a lot of channel-hogging cruisers if you knew the water. Over the years, it got so that I hardly bothered with the buoys at all, except at night. On Saturday night, it was de rigueur for a bunch of us to hop into our boats and head into town for the Big Dance. The runs home in the wee hours were memorable. You had to navigate by the sky line and the loom and reflection of the buoys on the water. You could use your flash light to pick them out, but that meant slowing down. Since there were usually two or three boats on your tail (those without running lights stuck particularly close, as they were using yours) it was deemed safer to keep the speed up. This made for some concentrated night navigation for the lead boat. As one fellow traveller put it, "If the owner of a certain point ever lops a certain branch off a certain pine, he's going to find an awful lot of boats piled up on his lawn come Sunday morning."

At any rate, after I joined the Canadian Coast Guard, I learned something about tending navaids. It is a real job of work and it has to be done right. If somebody goes aground because an aid is out of position, then the agency responsible for putting it there is just about the most unpopular outfit on the coast.

On a man-made waterway, of course, there are a few additional wrinkles. The first is the locks. Come opening day, regardless of the winter, ice pressure, changing water levels, ground freeze and thaw, and general wear and tear on the machinery, those locks have to work. All maintenance, replacement, and upgrading schedules must accommodate that fact. The second wrinkle is water levels. If the chart specifies a certain depth at a certain spot, boaters naturally assume that they will always find at least that depth there, and some of the larger craft shave the bottom pretty close as it is.

The longest skating rink in the world.

Obviously, all this does not just happen. Some agency has to make it so, which brings us to the good folks of the Rideau Canal, working out of beautiful downtown Smiths Falls. To see how they do it, we are going to follow them through a year of operation.

a) Winter. As soon as the navigation season ends, some sections of the system are drained down to their winter levels. This not only allows maintenance to be carried out on the locks, but also reduces ice pressure on the locks and walls. Furthermore, the low levels allow the system to accommodate some of the spring run-off. When it was decided to make the reach in Ottawa into

Buoy checking

the "Longest Skating Rink In The World", its level had to be raised a bit so that the ice would cover the full width of the canal. After skating is finished, the water is returned to its winter level.

Besides the locks, winter is also used for overhauling the marine plant, vessels, machinery and equipment.

b) Spring. The first step is to bring the water levels up to chart datum. The Canal uses the entire Rideau drainage basin as its reservoir, so a fine balance must be struck amongst getting rid of the excess run-off, flood control, current control, and maintaining an adequate reserve for the hot summer months.

As soon as water depth permits, the three maintenance craft get underway. These are low, flat decked vessels, 14.5 m (44 ft) in length, with a crane forward and a small wheel house aft. They also have mooring spuds (long posts that slide down through wells in the hull to the River bottom). What a great way to park. Put her in position, drop the spuds, and you don't shift a centimetre until you haul them up. The craft are powered by Harbourmaster outdrives, which allow them to nose into the banks for shore work. Their first task is to check all the aids in the system, to ensure they are exactly where they are supposed to be, and still in one piece after the winter's ice and storms. As there are 630 spar buoys, 109 day beacons, 5 lighted aids and dozens of speed control markers, this takes a lot of checking.

Rebuilding a gate

The Canal unlovingly calls these craft "scows". They are painted a sexy marine blue, which I suspect is a form of camouflage. If you can't pick them out on the water, you can't sidewalk superintend. I can't stand "scow", so I, all by myself, hereby reclassify them as "Navaids Tenders", and christen them MANOTICK, MERRICKVILLE, and MORTON BAY. There can be poetry in buoy lifting.

c) Navigational Season. A continuous eye must be kept on the water levels. Excessive rain has to be drained off, and this must be done carefully to avoid creating strong currents in the channel. Too dry a season means drawing down water from the reservoir lakes. Either way, the numbers must crunch out properly to maintain chart datum.

Out on the River, the three-person crews on each sco... NAVAIDS TENDER, dammit, are working the aids. These vessels are really mobile maintenance facilities which can lift the buoys right on deck to check and service the underwater portions, particularly the moorings. Buoys reaching the end of their days are replaced on site. The crews go ashore either directly from the beached vessel or via their small work boats to service

Lock repairs

or replace the beacons and signs, and clear any brush that is obstructing the sight lines.

d) Fall. After the system has closed down, the booms in front of the dams are lifted and floating docks and some floating speed signs are removed. The drain-down of some sections begins and the winter lock and plant overhaul programs get underway.

The Rideau Canal is a busy operation, the work barely noticed by passing boaters, but then efficient operations seldom are. So, say hello to the lockies as you go through, and if you see a strange blue object planing across the horizon at its usual 8 knots, give a wave to the crew. They are making sure you will have good sailing on their River.

Imagine the possibilities with those big flat-decked, er, whatchamacallems. Lash a couple together, add a boom box, some coolers, and what have you got? A typical staff meeting, that's what.

Installing lock gates

Lesson For To-day

1) The Waterway does not run by itself. Operating and maintaining it is a complex program carried out by a very competent group of people.

2) In order to help keep the system running smoothly, we, the users, can do our bit by navigating responsibly.

3) The Rideau people, besides being good at what they do, are a friendly and helpful bunch. We navigators can return the favour by being friendly and helpful to the world as well.

Now, let's say hello to our boating friends in the United States, particularly those who might be planning a cruise along our Waterway.

CHAPTER TEN
Welcome American Tourists

"Always HOLD THE MAP so that the part of the course to which you are going is farthest from you, like a road as you drive along it. This will make it much easier to follow, and prevent many mistakes."

—Dr. Lake

Over 150 years ago, we built the magnificent Rideau Waterway and it's all your fault. Back then, there was a fear that your ancestors might attack, and block, the St. Lawrence River, thus cutting my ancestors east of the Ottawa River off from those west of it. Since, as usual, they were barely talking to each other anyway, this would Not Be Good For National Unity. Therefore, the scheme was to build the Rideau system so that my ancestors could do an end run around your ancestors by sailing up the Ottawa and down the Canal. Since your ancestors never got around to invading, I presume they simply decided that it was much easier to just come as tourists. That way, they could bring their families, rather than the usual run of camp followers. It was a nice change for both sides.

Over the years, Americans who have come to Rideau country to cruise, fish, cottage, or just travel, have had a chance to see some of the most beautiful stretches of water in North America. Many have come back, and back again, some for generations.

To sail into a foreign land in your own craft can be an interesting experience. If you arrive at the Rideau via the Ottawa River, you will already have tasted navigation in Canada. Navigating up the Ottawa is simple. Just remember to speak English when

Early American tourists

talking to people on your port side and French when addressing people to starboard. You may or may not be ready for your first experience on the Rideau, which consists of being taken in your boat up the side of a cliff via the flight of eight Ottawa Locks in an ear-popping 1 1/4 hours. You then sail through a tunnel and fetch up in the heart of downtown Ottawa, awash with the very types of politicians you'd gone to sea to get away from in the first place. How's that for openers?

If you arrive via Kingston, you sail into port under the menacing guns of Fort Henry. You will observe that these guns are aimed at the State of New York. Canadian artillery doctrine has always been that, with a target that size, we're bound to hit something.

On arrival, your first duty will be to clear customs. In order to assist you with this, the following are some typical questions you could be asked, along with some suggested answers.

Customs Inspector: "Welcome to Canada. Lovely vessel you have there. The name is Terrence O'Shaunessy, and I'll be your Customs Inspector for to-day. While you are in the area, you might want to stop by the O'Shaunessy Gift Shop up the street, the O'Rourke Dry Goods Emporium on the next block, and O'Malley's Marine Supply along the shore. They all cater to American tourists. They'll even accept your dollars at par."

U.S. Boat: "Why, thank you for the suggestion. We've been looking forward to coming up here for some really great shopping."

C.I.: "Where are you folks coming from?"

U.S.B.: (Nodding to the south.) "The other side of the Lake."

C.I.: "Close enough. How long do you intend to stay in Canada?"

U.S.B.: "At least until our money runs out."

C.I.: "Right on. You can always send home for more. Do you have anything to declare?"

U.S.B.: " A couple of quarts, er, litres. Would you care for a nip?"

C.I.: "Well it is a bit fresh, (damp, hot, foggy, windy) this morning, (afternoon, evening, dawn). A small drop would be nice. (Downing a large one.) Thank you, and here are your clearance papers. As you have a left-handed boat hook on board, please study Section 729, Subsection 2c, Paragraph 14 - "Equipment - South Paws For The Use Of", before operating it. Have a pleasant trip."

As you proceed along the canal, besides seeing a moving waterscape of infinite variety, you will pass several towns and villages. Settlement of the valley followed a fairly set pattern. First would come an entrepreneur looking for a spot along the shore where the River flowed strongly enough to power a mill, either flour or lumber. The mill would go up along with a few homes and out-buildings. Then the battles with Col. By over water rights would begin. (If you are from one of the south-western states, you are probably familiar with the drill on water rights.) Often, the second structure to get built would be a distillery. We Canadians have our traditions, you know. With plenty of wood for building available in the bush, fish and game for the taking, and lots of flour and booze, the foundations of a solid, God-fearing community were then in place.

Some of the lock stations are guarded by block houses, an integral part of the Colonel's strategic plan. If your ancestors had attacked across the St. Lawrence, my ancestors would have carried out a phased withdrawal up the Rideau towards Ottawa. They were going to adopt a scorched earth policy until it was pointed out that there really wasn't much worth scorching back then. Instead, they calculated that, after working up a huge

U. S. boat

thirst attacking the block houses, and then quenching it at the distilleries, your ancestors would never make it to Ottawa. We knew our enemy. Napoleon could have learned a thing or two about strategic retreat from us.

There are two other things you should know about travelling in Canada. Firstly, the official currency is the Loonie. This coin was born out of one of those monumental bureaucratic boondoggles that periodically erupt in Ottawa and make being Canadian so much fun.

Canada has also gone metric. We don't add or subtract measurements anymore, we just move the decimal points around. However, except for speed limits, the Canal has not converted yet. That is down the road. They're probably just waiting until I can get my dream-boat. Then they'll trot out the new charts and confuse me all over again. Enjoy your voyage along the Rideau and thank your ancestors for kick-starting its construction. As with so many Government projects, it came in about 300% over budget, (close enough for Government work, as we say in Ottawa), and was never used for its intended purpose. However, boaters, both Canadian and American, know what to do with a fine waterway, even more so than the strategists. We have been rewarded by their efforts very well, these past 160 years. So come on over for some great cruising, and when you get to Kingston, Inspector O'Shaunessy will greet you at the wharf and see you in.

Lesson For To-day

1) It is interesting to see how the great plans of politicians and generals fall down when the people decide they really have better things to do. The Rideau was built as a defense against your attack, but we all decided to go cruising together instead.

2) We have our little quirks up here, or you have yours down there, depending from which side one is talking. In general, however, you'll quickly feel at home in our waters, except, of course, when you have to blow some Loonies on metric conversion books. So come on in, the water's fine.

We've covered a lot of ground since the Introduction, and now we should sum it all up, to see whether there are any GREAT TRUTHS underlying all this stuff, or is it just a common sense approach to getting organized for the River. The former has more sex appeal but this is, after all, a family book.

Most of it is pretty obvious, when you stop and think about it. The point of the book, therefore, is to get you to stop and think about it. Let's see what we've got.

CHAPTER ELEVEN
F.W.E.

"The directions given,...are sufficiently full and exact to guide you in perfect safety; but they will not do so if you do not follow them exactly."

—Dr. Lake

When a vessel enters port at the end of her voyage, she eases into her berth, and the lines are put ashore and made fast. Only then is the ship considered secure and the message can come down from the bridge, "F.W.E."-Finished With Engines. (You might, of course, prefer "F.W.A."-Finished With Author, but I'll pretend not to hear it.) After F.W.E., the voyage reports must be written up, summarizing the key events and lessons learned. Our voyage has been these chapters and now we must write up the report.

You don't have to plan, crew, fit and store as if you were off to the North West Passage to travel the Rideau. You can, without humongous preparation, actually have a reasonably enjoyable cruise, although you may waste some valuable time and miss a few things worth seeing and doing, including the fun of planning and the anticipation. Of course, if you have done the trip before, you should already know the drill.

However, I contend that good preparation pays off. As you study the Waterway, you get a feel for which parts are worth spending time in and which are not. By knowing what is available where, including things to see and do, time does not have to be wasted searching for it. If your craft is well prepared, well stored, and with a handy sized crew, you have a high degree of independence and flexibility. It reduces the number of times that you have to be somewhere at some time to do or get something. You have, as we like to say, more productive time.

It is unlikely that you will be battling Force 10 gales, or undertaking truly heroic rescue missions, however much you anticipate the thrill. The Rideau is a pretty civilized waterway. It is rather easy to navigate, the waters are mostly protected, and the sailing directions simple. However, this does not excuse you from preparing for emergencies, nor from knowing how to respond effectively to them. The very fact that you are prepared will ease your mind as you cruise. I have "stood into danger" on occasion, but usually with a pretty good idea of how I'm going to get out of it. This system has worked pretty well for me—so far.

You also won't have to face down gimlet-eyed lockies, challenging you at every transit. Lockies are just about the greatest, most helpful and most patient bunch of folks you ever want to meet. As for the Long Arm Of The Law tracking your every move, that only happens if you've earned its attention. Normally, it is probably the friendliest Arm one can find. Anytime they want to pull us over for a chat, we'll say "Welcome aboard." (What else can you say?) With any luck at all, however, they could be interested in purchasing a couple of autographed copies of a fantastic new book about navigating the Rideau.

Then, of course, there is the Rideau itself. It really does have everything that Dr. Lake attributes to it in his quote which opens Chapter One, and more. Colonel By built well. What other soldier would have had the foresight to know that, not only would his Canal have to meet the strategic and commercial requirements of the 19th Century, but also the pleasure craft requirements of the 20th? He also built his canal to last. It is to his credit that the Canal has never required any major alterations in over 150 years of continuous use. His Waterway is a magnificent cruising ground, complete with scenery, history, events, activities, and fish. What else could a real cruise want?

In sum, you can make a good voyage without a lot of preparation, but you will make a much better one, in all respects, if you do some serious planning and organization. For a normal vacation, you must divide your attention amongst transport, accommodation, and recreation. For the Rideau, it can all be focused on the boat. Since it provides both your transportation and accommodation, it can also do wonders for your travel budget. Like getting ready for a party, half the fun is in the anticipation.

Underway, the navigator is responsible for his/her crew and boat, and to other users of the Waterway, as well as the Waterway itself. Few excuses are acceptable should the navigator abrogate those responsibilities. If you use, you must protect. If you protect, you can enjoy.

A pretty civilized waterway

What it all adds up to is that the preparation, responsible navigation, and stretching of productive time lead to better cruising, more fun, and happy memories.

Final Lesson

All the lessons can be boiled down as follows:

1) You Can Have Too Many Friends. You can have crowds, or comfort, but seldom both.

2) Preparation Pays. Productive time can be lost if you forgot to, or didn't bother to, do something, or bring something, before you left the wharf. Besides, preparation feeds anticipation, and that's half the fun.

3) Responsible Navigation Pays. People's lives, well-being, and property are involved, and, as the River belongs to everybody, it has to be respected. Responsibility sits lightest on two types of navigators; those that are so ignorant or thoughtless that they just don't give a damn for anybody else, and those that

are so on top of the job that acing it is a matter of course. Pick your slot.

4) Emergencies Do Happen. Usually they can be resolved, but you want to be a part of the solution, not the problem. Be prepared.

5) Once You Get Out On The River, you know that the preparation was worth the trouble, because you are doing it right in a happy ship.

Now, students, it is your teacher's turn in the barrel. You are about to learn how I, your esteemed mentor, would go cruising down the Rideau. In honour of the occasion, comment should be kept muted, at least in my presence.

CHAPTER TWELVE
Your Teacher's Trip

"This better be good."

—The Ghost of Dr. Lake

Well, students, you've heard the teacher expound for these many pages on how you should organize your voyage. Of course, you've probably also heard the old adage that those who can, do, and those who can't, teach, but leave us not be distracted by irrelevancies. Let me rather explain how my wife and I would handle the trip. You may take notes if you wish.

It is safe to say that we would do all the things this book suggests, and more, for the very reasons raised in the Introduction. Our time on the water is valuable to us, and we don't want to waste any of it on unproductive activities, particularly if they can be avoided by proper preparation. Since the Rideau is closed from October to May, we certainly should not be pressed for planning time. What better way to spend the winter than by spreading the charts out on the floor and really getting to know them, thumbing through the material, checking over the gear and seeing what's new on the market, and taking in the museum at Smiths Falls to see what's where. Come spring time, we'd be off down the highway to check out the system from shore side. You call that work? Now, let the Teacher's planning begin.

1. Bodies
The Light Of My Life. This is to introduce my wife, Peg, mother of our two lovely children, (just ask them), and two not so lovely cats. Since we are all old friends by now, you can just call her Mrs. Gray. (We are somewhat dated, because after 27 years, we

are still on our first marriages.) Peg's avocation is nurse cum research assistant in a medical specialty. While regular nurses have manuals to follow, it is Peg's job to write them, and when one is on the leading edge of one's field, there are few people to turn to for advice. She has to get it right on her own. Natural common sense is a great asset in her line. If it don't look right, feel right, or smell right, it probably ain't right. This asset serves us equally well on the water, and I recommend that you ship a good stock for your own cruise. It is often in short supply on the River.

So Peg is the "people" on our voyage. We'll have others aboard for a few hours on the water, or an overnighter or two. Most would get bored with our cruising style, simply because we are the two nosiest people afloat. I mean, the chart may not show anything of interest in that bay over there, but how can we be sure unless we take a look? Using this philosophy, it took us two full days to voyage from Seeley's Bay to Westport, a direct distance of about 33 km (20.2 miles), but nothing was missed and new friends were made. Boredom is our official excuse for not inviting crowds, but in truth, we simply want to hog all the space for ourselves.

2. The Boat

In selecting our cruiser, we feel we have some advantages over veteran yacht people.

Experience. Since we have never owned a yacht, we are not wedded to any particular type, shape, size or power.

Price. Since we can't, at present, afford any kind of cruiser whatsoever, money is no object. Everything the heart desires shall be in our design.

Availability. It is immaterial that what we want has yet to be designed. When naval architects see the beauty of our scheme, they will leap into their lofts to put it on paper, knowing millions are at stake.

Purpose. While Peg and I are lay people at yacht design, we are the world's leading experts on the requirements for the comfort and well-being of a certain Mr. and Mrs. R.D. Gray. Indeed, the amount of painstaking time and effort that we have lavished on this enterprise over the past 27 years just boggles the mind. The

Boy Boat Jockey

only purpose of the craft, therefore, is to convey its occupants in a manner they intend to rapidly become accustomed to. It is also an advantage that as long as the boat fulfils that purpose, we really don't have to give a damn what anybody else thinks of it. If you are not constrained by style, all kinds of possibilities open up. The Joneses can relax. We won't be keeping up.

a) Hull and Power. What we have come up with is a pontoon boat. These are generally not used for cruising, but they certainly have the potential. That statement requires a certain leap of faith on our part, because we have had almost no time on them. The one spin we did manage to take was interesting. It was blowing about 30 k.p.h., with a current of perhaps 4 k.p.h. (This wasn't the Rideau.) Boy Boat Jockey was either going to learn this thing or wind up chasing himself down the river. We dipsy doodled up, down and across at full throttle, and then backed, filled and kept station on a buoy, amongst other exercises. We had no problem adjusting to the boat. However, as she was almost bare of equipment and stores, it was not a real trial of a cruising boat. In addition, I have talked to people who own such boats, and watched them on the water. I conclude that they handle somewhat differently from other craft, but then that applies to every boat I've ever driven, sailed, paddled or rowed. Pontoons simply mean a new set of quirks to adapt to.

Pontoon boats have two things going for them; lots of usable, flexible space, and versatility. Down on the Big Rideau, they are

101

Complete camping mode

apparently known as "party boats". I will leave it to the reader to decide if that might have had an influence on our selection. Our preliminary design model will be 6.7 m (20 ft) in length by 2.7 m (8 ft) in beam, which gives us a lot of area to work with. In addition, that width, and a low centre of gravity, will provide a very stable platform. It will ride on minimum 58 cm (24 in.) diameter pontoons, as the larger size will give us extra freeboard. They will be fully compartmentalized (baffled) to prevent complete flooding of a pontoon, and fitted with both keels and splash plates. The hull will be strongly built to last. Power will be about 60 kw (80 h.p.). We aren't speed demons, but we like a good reserve on the throttle.

b) Superstructure. The canopy will be deployable in 4 configurations:

■ Fully Down to give a completely open deck.

■ Dodger. The forepart raised 1 m (3 ft) to protect from spray.

■ Aft Section Fully Raised to cover the control console and after seating. A screen can be hung in front to protect from rain and bugs.

■ Complete Camping Mode enclosing the whole deck.

c) Accommodation. As Peg puts it, "If he doesn't get his 40 winks, the next day he is tired, cranky, poor company, and a lousy lover. However, if he does get a good night's sleep, he is not tired." Accurate to a fault, that woman, but her diplomacy! Our bunk will, therefore, be a fold-out queen-size, with a mosquito netting canopy. The rest of our digs will consist of a single unit galley with propane and water systems, ice coolers, a chemical powder room, and roomy storage lockers with cushion covers for seating. The centre-forward area will be left clear, to be used as the occasion requires. I mean, why should my lady have to perch on an ordinary seat like any commoner, when it would befit her station much more if she had a suitably cushioned lounge chair, properly fitted to the tie-downs. From this point of vantage, an imperious wave back to the helm will serve to have the course changed, the speed adjusted, the glass recharged. Such things must be done in a fit and proper manner.

d) Tender. The dinghy will be a 2 m (6.5 ft) outboard-powered rigid-hull inflatable slung from stern-mounted davits.

e) Versatility. A boat like this, fully fitted, would weigh less than 1 metric ton, which could be towed by a 6-cylinder vehicle. With her canopy down, she would have little sail area, and her dimensions would be within Ontario highway limits. This means that she could be launched and recovered anywhere along the system, which gives us an infinite choice of voyages to make.

A second point is that a tent trailer is a tent atop a trailer. Our unit will be a tent atop pontoons atop a trailer, which just means 1 or 2 more steps to climb to get into it. Therefore, if we have a long road trip to reach the launching ramp, we can ease into a trailer park and set up for the night.

3. Preparations

We would do all the things, fit all the things and store all the things set out in Chapters One to Four. We would also add a few wrinkles of our own.

a) Ports Of Call Book. We would have a note book covering all ports along the way. It would briefly describe them under the general headings of fuel, maintenance, stores, things to do and see, and other. Then, if we want something we won't have to waste time hunting for it.

b) Layovers. We would want the names of some hotels and motels along the way that are near our berths and have full bathrooms. The idea is to lay over at one every 5 or 6 days and give the bodies, clothes, linens, etc. a good going over. The boat can also be swept out and the equipment and stores checked. This is easier to do if the stuff can be spread out on a wharf and unpacked.

4. The Voyage

Whither And When. Assuming we had two weeks, we would aim to get underway in the third week in August, when traffic starts to thin out. Since we live in Ottawa, we would start from Mooney's Bay. The car would be left in our driveway, with the trailer hooked on, and a driver detailed off to come fetch us from wherever. Our speed would take us through the duller reaches, leaving us lots of time to loaf in the interesting areas. We don't cruise to a fixed schedule if we can help it. After Kingston, we would mooch along the St. Lawrence for a few days to check out the bootleggers and other touristy stuff. Then we would check our time line, and decide whether to call for pick-up or keep on motoring.

Along the way, we would have a few family and friends join us from time to time, stop and talk to people, swing around the hook when the mood strikes us, take away the tender for a little exploring, swim, read and day-dream.

Finally, we would be responsible navigators. It certainly won't cost us in time, money, effort or enjoyment to do so, and leaving the River in as good a shape as we found it, and the people as friendly as when we met them, are good investments. We, and probably our kids some day, will be back for more.

If, as we cruise, we should happen upon one of those newly christened navaids tenders, why we'll simply sidle up, lash together, and, ignoring the cries of "Repel boarders!", break out the boom box and coolers. Then, we'll inquire if they are interested in purchasing a couple of autographed copies of a fantastic new book about navigating the Rideau.

F.W.E.

ACKNOWLEDGEMENTS

It is a daunting exercise for a fledgling author to submit a manuscript such as this for technical review. The reviewers are a select group, with extensive knowledge, experience and interest in marine operations in general and the Rideau in particular. They have a range of backgrounds, which has given me a wide variety of perspectives.

The reviewers each quite properly took the position that, if I am going to write about their River, it behove them to make sure I got it right. Totally ignoring this fledgling's more tender sensibilities, they spent considerable time and effort to setting me straight. The result, I believe, has become a distillation of the thinking of some of the most knowledgeable minds on the subject of boating on the Rideau. They are:

Ballinger, D.	Assistant Superintendant, Rideau Canal, and his staff.
Elliot, P.	Friends Of The Rideau Association.
Greenham, M.S.	Captain, Canadian Coast Guard and Rideau navigator.
Mather, B.	Fishing and hunting guide and trapper, Rideau Waterway.
Mattila, K.	Rideau property owner and Rideau navigator.
McCurdy, I.	Senior Constable, Marine Patrol, Ontario Provincial Police and Rideau navigator.
Millar, F.A.S.	Captain, Canadian Coast Guard and Rideau navigator.
Sosnick, R.	Lockmaster, Beveridges Lockstation.
Taylor, W.	Past Vice Commodore, and presently, Chairman, Government Liaison, Canadian Power and Sail Squadron. Rideau navigator.

These men have my appreciation for their input. I hope that anybody who has learned anything from this book will equally value their contributions.

Having all this magnificent expertise at my disposal did not, however, excuse me from the responsibility of producing a useful manuscript. I have laced these pages with a considerable amount of opinion, asides, stories, wisecracks and other insertions, for which these reviewers bear no responsibility, particularly as they don't happen to agree with all of them. This is the way it should be. If, God forbid, mariners started to agree with each other all the time, conversation in their pubs wouldn't be worth listening to.

A guide such as this is not worth much if the uninitiated can't follow it. Three such people agreed to check out this aspect. I want to thank Mr. and Mrs. P. Murray, who cheerfully admit that their rather incomplete knowledge of boating and the Rideau eminently qualifies them for this task, and my wife Peg. She properly feels that she has no need to understand the operation of boats. Her navigator is supposed to know all about that stuff.

DEAR READER:

I hope you enjoyed reading this book. Lord knows, you paid good money for the thrill. At any rate, if you liked it, and more important, picked up a few pointers to help you go cruising, you should have satisfaction. I certainly enjoyed the research and writing. It's nice to be able to say to even the most skeptical shoresider, "Hey! I have to go out on the River to-day. It's my job. I'll come by your office and see you when it's raining." It was tough, I tell you, but it had to be done.

When it came to the writing, I tried not to think in terms of me at my little word processor generating a Great Tome for you to burn the midnight oil over. Rather, I imagined a bunch of us down at the wharf one day. "Hey Doug," one of you would open, "some of us are thinking of cruising down the Rideau, but we're not to sure how to go about it." "Well, the way I see it," I would reply, "if you want to do it right, you oughta start by..." and off we'd go, working out your trip.

Whether it actually comes out like that in the book, I'll leave you to judge. In signing off, I appreciate having passed some time in your company and hope to see you out on the River one day.

Bon Voyage,

Doug

BIBLIOGRAPHY OF NAVIGATION

Lake, Dr. E.J.   *Chart Of The Rideau Lakes Route*
Third Edition. Reprinted by The Rideau
District Museum, 1990

Canadian Parks Service-Rideau Canal:
Historic Canals - Fees And Hours Of Operation
Rideau Canal Between Kingston And Ottawa
Locking Through Safely
Rideau Canal Navigation Data
Heritage Canal Regulations, plus 1987 and 1990 Amendments

Canadian Coast Guard:
Small Vessel Regulations
Safe Boating Guide
Directory Of Safe Boating Information
Collision Regulations
Boating Restriction Regulations
The Canadian Aids To Navigation System

Canadian Hydrographic Service:
Rideau Waterway Chart 1512. Ottawa To Smiths Falls (3 sheets)
                 Chart 1513. Smiths Falls To Kingston (5 sheets)
Small Craft Guide. Rideau Waterway And Ottawa River Notices
To Mariners
Guide To Federal Small Craft Harbours - Ontario

Department Of Communications:
A Guide For The Maritime V.H.F. Operator

The Canadian Red Cross Society;
Know Your Power Boat
Cold Water Survival
Your P.F.D. Is Your Protection. Wear It!
Anglers And Hunters Safe Boating Guide

Ontario Ministry Of Natural Resources:
Sharing Our Waterways
Don't Rock The Boat
Pleasure Boating In Ontario
Boating Regulations And Information 1991
Zebra Mussels

Ontario Ministry Of The Environment:
Marine Pump Out Stations
Grey Water Disposal From Pleasure Boats
Spills Response Program

Commercial:
Nissan Marine: Don't Make Waves
Ontario Marina Operations Association: Marinas
Zurich Canada: Seamanship

BIBLIOGRAPHY OF TOURISM

Legget, R.	*Rideau Waterway.* 2nd. Edition University Of Toronto Press. 1986
Parks Canada	*Rideau Boating And Road Guide 1988*
Rideau Trail Assoc.	*Rideau Trail Notes. 1981*
	Map Kit
Lanark County Tourist Assoc.	*Going Places*
O.M.P.A.	*The Tourist Guide Book Of Ontario* 1991-92 Edition
Kalman and Roof	*Exploring Ottawa* 1987

The following is an excellent source work covering all aspects of the Rideau Canal and the Rideau Valley.

Turner, L.	*Rideau Canal Bibliography. 1972-92* Friends Of The Rideau. Commonwealth Historic Resources Management, Ltd.

RELATED BOOKS FROM GSPH

OUR RIVER, THE RIDEAU ....$ 6.50
(Plus $2.00 for shipping, handling & GST)

THE RIDEAU SHORELINE.......................................$14.95
(Plus $3.00 for shipping, handling & GST)